Original
Wisdom

D1379448

Original

Stories of an Ancient Way of Knowing

Wisdom

ROBERT WOLFF

INNER TRADITIONS
Rochester, Vermont

Inner Traditions International
One Park Street
Rochester, Vermont 05767
www.InnerTraditions.com

Library of Congress Cataloging-in-Publication Data

Wolff, Robert.
    Original wisdom : stories of an ancient way of knowing /
Robert Wolff.
        p. cm.
    ISBN 0-89281-866-2 (pbk.)
      1. Ethnophilosophy. 2. Ethnopsychology. 3. Human ecology.
4. Senoi
(Southeast Asian people) I. Title.

GN468 .W65 2001
305.8'001—dc21

                                                      2001002723

Printed and bound in Canada

10 9 8 7 6 5 4 3 2 1

Text design and layout by Cindy Sutherland
This book was typeset in Classical Garamond with Centaur as
display typeface.

To my sons, too young
to share much of my life as I lived these stories,
but you were in my heart;

To the friends who have encouraged me to go on,
while putting up with my doubts and indecisions,
and also to those who wished me ill,
from whom I learned about compassion and nonviolence;

And to wonderful friends all over the world,
in Suriname, Indonesia, Malaysia, the Philippines,
and on many islands of the Pacific,
who helped me learn to feel human again.

Author's Note

Events described in this book are not fiction. However, they are filtered through both time and my point of view.

Most of the dialogue is my free translation of the original language(s) spoken. My intention has been to preserve some of the flavor and color of the original.

Contents

Foreword

Most of us were raised in the Empire of the First World, a world and culture steeped in literacy, certain of the fundamental truth that life's great goal is to find that niche where we can spend our days working to the larger enrichment of another person or corporation.

When we hear or read of people who live a more idyllic life in a laterally organized culture without layers of hierarchy or riches or want, we tend to think of them as either mythological or, if real, simply too ignorant to have developed civilization. Indeed, with books such as *The Ecological Indian* there is a worldwide movement afoot today to "prove" that indigenous peoples were every bit as wanton, rapacious, and planet-destructive as are we (albeit they were less technically competent).

And certainly some were. But such generalizations always fail; it's as if we were to try to describe all Europeans by the story of the Roma Gypsies or Attila's Huns.

It's even fashionable nowadays for First World ecotourists to visit remote parts of the world, spend a week or two with an indigenous shaman, smoke a few plants, see a few hallucinations, then come back to declare themselves shamans and develop large followings. Shamanism for self-growth, shamanism for business, shamanism to build wealth and power—it's popping up all over, but always with a curiously familiar flavor since it's simply the most recent reinvention of the classic dominating leader/searching follower, you-pay-me-and-I-teach-and-lead-you way so many cults, fads, and religions have gone.

For those who have never learned the language of indigenous peoples, true contact is impossible, for the culture is embedded in the language. Ecotourists meet natives or guides who have already been culturally contaminated simply by learning to talk with us. Their worldview has been shifted by contact, and their hungers often tend toward metal, TV, candy, alcohol, and guns. So how is one to know what's true?

The question is important, because those of us with European or African or South American roots have ancestors who lived as indigenous, tribal people for the vast majority of the history of the human race. Yet nobody in Europe today remembers the Old Ways, the sacred places and plants, the meanings of the stones and markings and holy groves. It was all wiped out in a massive holocaust led first by the Celts, then the Romans, and then the Catholic Church. And that great forgetting was then carried to five other continents by zealous missionaries, the first wedge of empire and theft, and brutally enforced by armies and trading companies for five centuries.

Now comes Robert Wolff. Trained as a psychologist with a smattering of anthropology, but possessing the heart and soul of an aboriginal Malay, he learned the language of the secretive Malaysian jungle people, the Sng'oi. A few books have been written about them, often dismissed as fanciful and one even as fictional, but none written (to the best of my knowledge) by people who actually lived among them and spoke their language.

But Robert Wolff did.

Through that experience he discovered a startling new reality, a new way of knowing, which is largely missing from the lives of modern Americans and Europeans, and when mentioned is often relegated to the fringes of science by our religious empiricists.

But the reality—and the profundity—of his experience cannot be escaped. This book will fascinate you in its reading and haunt you in its memory. Most important, it will fill you with hope for a human future more in line with what it means to truly be human.

Read it, dream about it, and share it with your friends. This is a message the world must hear.

Thom Hartmann
Montpelier, Vermont

Introduction

As I am preparing this collection for publication again I think back to my childhood. I grew up in a very small town in Sumatra. My family—mother, father, and one sister—was small, but we lived among a dozen people and their families who helped us live a rich and comfortable life. Those people I thought of as *my other family*. During the hottest part of the day, when we were supposed to rest, I often joined them as they sat around in the shade, sharing gossip and stories. The stories were fables, I knew, but even after many retellings they never lost their wonder. Over the years fables became lessons that began to tell me what the world "out there" might be like. Even now, so many years later, I hear the rhythm of the Malay language, I see people sitting around, leaning against a pole or against each other. Life was never hurried. I learned without being aware that I did. I still remember the time when it dawned on me that relations between humans can be very complicated and difficult, but nevertheless it was impressed upon me that humans always exist within a larger context. I knew that people, despite great differences, are related as humans, as we are related to the animals and plants around us.

Now I am an elder myself. The fables I heard when I was a child have faded into the background of stories I have lived, my own stories that continue their life within me— wherever it is that stories are kept.

A number of years ago I began to write down a few of these and then put some of them together in a book, which I published in 1994. The book found its own readers; I never marketed it. Now, a new version of this collection may find its way to a larger audience.

✠   ✠

My life has spanned what must be a unique period in the long history of humankind: a period of immense changes worldwide. The human population of the world has more than doubled in the last forty years; we have pumped more oil out of the ground after World War II than in all history before then. In the last fifty years, the millions of cars and millions of miles of roads we have built, and that have become commonplace, have changed the face of the planet forever. An ever-growing number of humans has access to facilities and luxuries kings could not have dreamed of even fifty years ago.

Westerners, who are in the vanguard of these changes, see them as progress, an assumption rarely questioned.

Perhaps because my perspective includes memories of a kinder, gentler world, I have become acutely aware of what we have lost. In our haste to create a world entirely based on artificial—that means man-made—*things,* we have thrown away much that is part of our heritage as creatures of this planet. By divorcing ourselves from Nature we have also removed ourselves from the wisdom that comes from living as part of What Is.

In this age it is not unusual anymore to visit and even live in faraway lands. We travel halfway around the earth for a week's vacation or for an assignment of a few months. Where French was the language of diplomacy not all that long ago, English has become the language of world trade. Tourists travel to outlying islands to find the perfect beach, or to an exotic big city for bargains.

And yet it seems that the easier it becomes to travel, the more difficult it is to meet people in their own world.

I feel blessed to have been able to meet the people who changed my life, a tribe of aborigines in Malaysia. In some ways they reminded me of the people I knew as a child, but they were more primitive. I can easily imagine that they are a rare remnant of humans as we used to be a few thousand years ago.

After leaving Malaysia, where we lived for a few years, I began to read all I could find written by travelers and scientists who had known other aboriginal people. The more I read, the more I realized that Bushmen and Pygmies in Africa, Eskimos in the high Arctic, Australian aborigines, and isolated tribes here and there around the world were described in very much the same words: peaceful, nonviolent, nonaggressive. All the aboriginal people who survived into the twentieth century lived in areas of scarce resources: dense jungles, arid deserts, snow-swept ice fields. They lived in isolation, far from civilization. They were shy. They were nomadic, with few possessions, and their communities did not have elaborate hierarchies of power. And there was something else these groups had in common: they could not be "tamed," to borrow the word

Laurens van der Post uses to write about the Bushman of the Kalahari Desert.

I wondered what it was that affected me so deeply about the Sng'oi of Malaysia. Certainly, they had a kind of integrity that I had not sensed in other people. I loved their joyfulness, their ability to be in the present, their utter simplicity. When I was with them I was moved by the strange synchronicities (C. G. Jung's term) that so often occurred. How was it possible that people without a telephone knew that I was coming to visit, when I did not know myself until a few hours before I left home? How could one person know what another was thinking and feeling and dreaming? But perhaps more than anything else, with the Sng'oi I basked in a kind of unconditional love that is rare in Western societies and in societies that have become Westernized. I now know that I could find them only if they wanted to be found. They trusted me.

My love for a people who experienced reality directly, rather than through layers of learned concepts of what the world *should* be, allowed me to rediscover a reality of my own that is as immediate and intimate as the world of the Sng'oi. I recognized that I had hidden this reality deep inside myself. I had always known that the world and I were inseparably *one*, but had suppressed that knowing, buried it under words and theories.

My friends the Sng'oi, and others of these stories, helped me regain the reality of being *part* of All-That-Is.

Westerners are intolerant of other ways to organize society, other ways to be human. We cannot accept that others may value different ways of being. We seem to be stuck in the idea that all people must want what we have and what we value—all those things that we believe prove that Western civilization is the pinnacle of human achievement, the best, the future.

Science is so sure that it is the only truth that it has become incapable of accepting other ways of learning about reality. Medicine, as a scientific discipline, for instance, is certain that all other forms of healing are quackery and are not to be tolerated; they must be rooted out, destroyed. Such arrogant insistence has eradicated much knowledge and wisdom in the world.

I always knew that there were other, older ways of healing.

For many years my work took me to many parts of Southeast Asia and the Pacific. I recorded and collected what I could of methods of healing and herbal medicines. I became obsessed with the thought that I ran a race with time, that soon it would be too late because no one would remember ancient traditions. It seemed that all such knowledge was being erased by our intolerance of other-ness. I was deeply saddened by what I believed was an irreparable loss. In our rush to create man-made chemicals, we rejected age-old knowledge of the riches of the earth that are freely available all around us. We invented machines, but ignored talents and abilities we must have in our very genes.

My agony over what I thought of as a great loss stayed with me until one day when I was in Tonga, an island kingdom in the South Pacific (Tonga is one of the few countries that have escaped colonization, although not the overlay of a Western religion). I mentioned my despair over what we had lost to a woman who had been pointed out to me as a gifted native healer. So much knowledge and wisdom, I said, was lost through our crude but persistent efforts to eradicate native cultures.

She thought about that for a long time. Finally she said, "Yes, I know what you mean. Yes, we too used to have healers and much knowledge of healing and herbs. Most of that is gone."

She paused again for at least a minute, then she sat up straight and looked me in the eye, her voice becoming stronger and more affirmative: "But"—and she pointed her finger for emphasis—"that is not the whole of it. You see, there have always been people who know. When we most need it, someone will remember that ancient knowledge."

She sat back, smiling. "So you see, traditions may be lost, but the information is in here and in here," she said, pointing to her head, then her heart, "and when we need it most, it will be inside us, for us to find."

She was referring to herself, I knew. Her gift of healing did not come from a Western education, nor did it come from training in traditional healing. It came from within.

I must believe what she said is true. I have experienced that *knowing*. There were times when I needed knowledge of the plants around me—and it came to me. Instinctively I knew where to find the knowledge (now we would say information) I needed.

The same is true in other areas of skill and experience. The ancient art of building canoes may have been lost, but when I was a passenger traveling on the open ocean in a fourteen-foot Boston whaler for twelve hours with no land in sight, the sailors who manned the vessel remembered again how to find their way by the stars at night, and during the day by the currents and "the little winds," as some Polynesians say. It is true that what remains of old traditions is no longer a coherent system of knowledge and skills, yet individuals everywhere are rediscovering and re-creating what their forebears had.

There are *kahuna* (priests) again in Hawai'i. A century ago, missionaries did what they could to eradicate all remnants of heathenism, but somehow enough ancient knowledge survived. I knew a modern-day kahuna well; he considered himself a *kahuna lapa'au*, a healing priest. He agreed that what he knew did not always come to him in a straight line, from father to son, from teacher to pupil, but rather from his own knowing—from inside himself. Others have said the same.

Perhaps, despite great destruction of human experience, ancient insight and wisdom are not lost. Somehow they are still part of us, inside us. These insights can and will come back to us when we need them.

✠ ✠

As a child listening to the people who were near and dear to me, I never thought that one way of looking at the world was better than another. When I returned to that part of the world as an adult I realized that our arrogant attitude toward other ways of being caused great pain, and eventually the destruction of almost all indigenous cultures in these latter years.

That was brought home to me most searingly when I visited a small island in the Pacific with a few coworkers. I had no part in the job the public health people had to do that day, so I asked one of the local people to show me

around the island. I told him that I was particularly interested in learning about what I called native medicine.
When he seemed doubtful I explained that, obviously, people who had lived on a small island, far away from other
islands, must have developed ways to heal wounds.
Certainly they must know how to assist in childbirth—perhaps even know ways to set a broken bone. "Oh that," he
said, "yes, there are some people who know."

We walked around the island. He introduced me to a
woman who knew herbs, and to two sisters who were mid-
wives. We met a man who knew which of the many different kinds of seaweed could be used medicinally, and several
people who had other healing skills.

I took copious notes, although I soon discovered that
people were not happy when I made notes in their presence. So between visits, my guide and I would sit on a rock
somewhere and I would write in my notebook. We talked.

It was afternoon when we came back to where the boat
waited for us to take my friends back to the main island, and
to take me back to the airport. The island did not have a harbor or much of a beach, so we had to be ferried to the boat
in local canoes. I was in the last canoe. Just as we were about
to manhandle the canoe into the water, my guide of the day
rushed up with a gift. He wanted to thank me, he said
breathlessly:

"You are the first [white man] who said some things we
have is worth."

His words made an indelible impression on me. I realized
that what he said was probably true. Other white men may
have visited his island, but nobody had ever taken the trouble to ask them about their lives, their practices, their

beliefs, their knowledge—because we are so sure that whatever indigenous people have is not worth knowing.

The stories in this book are true in the sense that I lived them. I share them to honor the worth and wisdom of the many people I came to know all over the world.

Assumptions

My first career position was government psychologist in Suriname, a developing country in South America. I had worked before, of course, but this, I thought, would be the first step on my career ladder. Little did I know that this ladder not only went up, but it also went around the world.

While we were in Suriname, *Life* magazine photographed the jungles around Paramaribo, the capital city, for what later became the issue on the tropical rain forest in the series "The World We Live In." The country lies a few degrees above the equator. It is hot and humid and densely forested. Then, there were few roads—one traveled on the rivers in steamboats or dugout canoes.

Suriname had been a colony first of England, then of Holland, and now had a new sort of independence. The original population was Native Caribbean American. They call themselves Arawak. They were displaced by African slaves a few hundred years ago. Because of the dense jungle, a majority of slaves escaped almost immediately and were never captured. Instead, these slaves who liberated themselves established a seventeenth-century African culture in the interior of Suriname. A hundred years ago they made peace with the government of the Netherlands. The Djuka, as they called themselves then, controlled the interior; the Dutch ruled a narrow strip along the coast, with the capital, Paramaribo, and a few other small towns. Today Suriname is independent.

The colonists were certain that they were unable to work in that climate. They were probably right: they wore too many clothes for a tropical jungle, but they also thought themselves vastly superior to people who did not have their kind of civilization. So workers had to come from elsewhere. After the abolition of slavery, people from South Asia (now India, Pakistan, Bangladesh, and Sri Lanka) and later from Java could be talked into signing contracts as indentured laborers. Although the contracts guaranteed that they would be returned home after their term was served, many chose to stay.

In Suriname all people mixed indiscriminately. The palette of skin colors there is unique in the world. There may be few African blacks (also called blue-blacks), but there is, every other shade of black, brown, beige, yellow, and almost-white.

Suriname has aluminum ore that is mined by ALCOA, the United States aluminum company. Some people worked for ALCOA, a few people grew food—and a few even found gold nuggets in the jungle and smuggled them to Miami—but there was not much of anything people could do to make a living, except work for the government, the largest employer in the country at that time.

Very soon after we arrived I heard that some of the department heads and other bosses felt that workers were lazy and unambitious. That surprised me because people I had befriended seemed happy, active men and women, always ready to improve themselves. Since there was no institution of higher learning in the country, they wrote away for correspondence courses. It was only later that I learned that my friends often took courses that had little or nothing to do with their work. But the students felt they were improving *themselves,* not their work skills. They desperately wanted to learn and they found learning where they could.

After I was hired I was asked, What does a psychologist do? I had two degrees in psychology, one of them a brand-new, untested degree in social psychology from a famous American university. I thought I knew survey technology; I was supposed to know how to construct, conduct, analyze, and interpret an "attitude survey." So when I was asked what a psychologist does, I explained attitude surveys, sampling, research in general, the importance of validity and reliability—none of which was an answer to the question, of course. Then I said that a psychologist finds out what people are *really* like, not what other people think they are like.

Undoubtedly I explained too much. I got no reaction. I thought the subject closed. In fact, I almost forgot about it.

Someone knew, however, that psychologists also administer tests. I was put to work testing children in a newly established child guidance clinic. My first official action had to be telling my superior that we could not use any of the tests he had ordered because the tests were designed for Western-educated children. Local children spoke a different language, had a very different culture, and could not be expected to be within norms developed elsewhere.

We invented other tests and we managed.

✠　✠

About a year later, when I had almost forgotten my earlier conversation about what a psychologist does, a notice in the local paper screamed: *The Government hereby announces that the Government Psychologist will conduct a scientific study to find out why people are so lazy. All people are notified that they must cooperate!*

I protested. I tried to make my superiors understand that under the circumstances I could not do a valid study. They agreed to wait six months, while I carefully and secretly designed a survey and hoped people would forget the notice in the newspaper.

Our survey would ask a sample of government employees questions about their attitudes toward work. When we did a trial run, we discovered that few people had ever taken a multiple-choice test. Our trial run failed miserably. I revised my ideas and designed an interview study. We changed the questions somewhat and trained interviewers.

Through this we discovered that it was not the format after all, but the *questions* that were wrong. Too many people could not answer the questions our interviewers asked. For instance, after a section in which interviewers asked employees what their jobs were (by jobs *we* meant careers), we asked, "If you were not doing what you are doing now, what would you prefer to do?" A common enough question in the West, which I expected would lead people to express their satisfaction with their job, and perhaps even their motivation and ambition.

Instead I was met with blank stares.

To our question they responded, "What I am doing now." They asked, What else would we be doing? Yes, definitely, what they were doing now.

✠　✠

At the children's clinic, meanwhile, I had been trying to use a test that was commonly used in Europe and America at that time. I would give the children a plain piece of paper and some colored crayons and ask them to draw something, anything.

To my astonishment, of the children who were given the test (263, at first), only two produced anything at all. The rest sat with dead faces. Ages varied, but all the children were primary-school-age. Their average age was eight and a half.

The Draw Something, Anything test had been discussed extensively in psychology books and journals; there were established norms to interpret the work that children would produce. The test was considered to be cross-cultural; it could be used in any culture without bias, the experts said. And yet here was a population where children between the ages of six and ten years did not produce anything that could be analyzed.

I thought of several explanations. Perhaps paper and pencil were strange to them (I was wrong about that). Or, I thought, they were scared of me, because I am white. I got along with the children well enough and had never sensed any fear in them, but in a country of people of all imaginable colors, few were as white as I am. I asked a native teacher to help me administer the test. She asked the children to draw something, anything.

Same result: blank stares.

✳   ✳

When my family and I made friends, we were struck by the many possible configurations of families. They were only sometimes made up of father, mother, and children, and were much more likely something else. We knew a mother and twelve children who had varying arrangements with at least four of the children's fathers. While these men were not live-in parents, they were considered family and they regularly visited the mother's large home. Another family we knew occupied three adjacent houses. There were three grandmothers, two grandfathers, fathers, mothers, countless aunts, uncles, a colorful (and powerful) grandaunt, nieces and nephews, cousins—and, of course, many children. I never learned who the head of that family was, but as we got to know them, it seemed as if there were several separate webs of relationships and decision making that were hard to comprehend. The young woman who managed the money in that family became a special friend of ours. When we asked her how many people were in her family, she threw up her hands and said, "I never know from one day to the next. People come and go."

Few people in Suriname were rich because, in part, it is almost impossible to become rich when the money that is coming in is shared by such large extended families. Yet nobody in that large group went hungry.

All of these different kinds of families seemed to have in common that they wished fervently for their children to improve themselves. Improving yourself did not mean learning a particular skill, but becoming more knowledgeable in general, becoming, perhaps, more cultured.

But I am getting ahead of my story. I did not fully realize the importance the families attached to improving oneself until after the results of the survey.

❈　❈

The survey was barely limping along when a man came to see me. Although uneducated, he was obviously intelligent and insightful. He said that because he thought I liked the country's people, he wanted to help me.

"It is very simple," he said. "People here have not had much choice about anything. We do not think in terms of what we would rather be doing. When a boy reaches the age when it is thought that he'd better do something to stay out of trouble, the first job that comes along is what he does. When it is time for him to get a woman, the first woman that comes along, who is willing, is his woman."

Very simple, indeed.

Immediately I made the obvious connection with the Draw Something, Anything test. What would happen, I wondered, if I asked the children to draw a house, or their mother, or themselves? They all drew with gusto and no little skill. All along it was not that they could not draw, what blocked them was my instruction to draw something, anything. They needed to be told *what* to draw. The children had no difficulty expressing themselves, imagining, creating, but they had never been given that much choice, that much freedom.

I discussed this with teachers and others. Yes, they all agreed, the culture, the way people had been living, did not allow many choices, so that such an open-ended direction to draw something, anything might well be meaningless to the children, perhaps even frightening.

I can choose between carrots and tomatoes if both vegetables are on a dish in front of me. But when there is only one vegetable, and from past experience I know that is all there is, it would be foolish for me to say what I would rather have. I take what is offered.

Now I understood the stares we received when we asked some of the questions on the survey. They had never been asked those kinds of questions before. People had never thought about what they would *rather* do. They did whatever work there was. Because choosing was not something people had much practice with, choosing an imaginary alternative was simply not in their experience.

✠ ✠

The survey became a much larger project than I had foreseen. I had to reconsider questions that would have been routine if we had done this survey in a Western country. This was not a Western country, however.

We could no longer ask what people would rather do. Instead we read them little stories, with the idea that by identifying with the people in the story, they could tell us what they thought the people in the story would choose. After doing some trial tests, that seemed to work well enough.

In the end, when we had rewritten the questions several times, when we thought we had good, reliable information, when we had analyzed all the information forward and backward . . . I found that it was the questions *I had asked myself* that were wrong. I had made assumptions about human behavior that might have made sense in a Western society, but they made no sense in Suriname at that time.

Of course, Surinamers were not lazy—far from it. They sacrificed their own time and money to take correspondence courses. True, the courses they took often had no bearing on their jobs, but acquiring new or better job skills was not why they took them.

I had assumed that workers thought as Westerners do: the better you do a job, the more income you will get. Therefore it is to your advantage to learn things that help you do a better job. I assumed that was how people everywhere thought about work. These assumptions are so basic in our society that we are not aware that we hold them. In Suriname at that time, however, your worth was not determined by what you did, or how well you did it, but by your becoming a better person.

Most families we knew wanted the children to become better people. They had not learned that in a Western world it does not pay to acquire a general education, but it is important to have better training for a specific job.

Someone told me, "It is not so much what you have [training, skill, or even money] that determines your worth, but who you are [a good person]."

✠ ✠

In tribal societies one's worth comes from the tribe one belongs to, not from individual skills or competence. In Suriname, government employees knew, of course, that they no longer lived in a tribal society, but they felt that they now belonged to the government. They were proud to belong to the government, which they called *papa govn'men*. It was a prestigious tribe to belong to. And to show their pride as well as their appreciation, they took correspondence courses to better themselves. You did your tribe proud by becoming a better person.

It did not occur to people that an employer might not care whether you were a better person. The employer was interested in hiring a better-qualified employee, or a better-educated employee, or a more ambitious employee who might acquire new job-related skills.

The expectations of employer and employee were very different. Employers grumbled because employees were lazy, they said, or unambitious. But the behavior they judged lazy or unambitious was rooted in tribal thinking. Employers thought as Westerners think. Employers lived in one reality, the reality of the West. Employees lived in a very different reality: the reality of a tribal people.

❋   ❋

Some years later I met a very sophisticated university professor from Suriname's neighboring country Guyana. He was bitter and quite outspoken about what he called the colonial experience: "Their [the colonists] whole culture is designed to imprint on us [the colonized] that they are better than we. They tell us that we must strive to become like them, lords and ladies. But we cannot become lords and ladies. We shall always be less."

He spoke impeccable, immaculate BBC English. If you had not seen his dark brown skin, you certainly might have thought him Lord something or other.

Surinamers, perhaps, felt *less* as well, and perhaps believed that improving themselves would buy entry into the civilized world.

❋   ❋

I learned that I cannot make assumptions about what drives people, nor can I make generalizations about what people are really like, until I can stand in their shoes, so to speak.

My apologies to the blank-faced children whom I asked to draw something, anything. They had not learned to choose. They never had to choose—there had been few possibilities for choices in their lives.

Draw Something, Anything

It is a long way from a world with few choices to our world with too many choices, and new choices emerging every day. Choosing has come to be one of the central aspects of our Western way of life. We cannot do anything, go anywhere, without having to choose. What shall I wear? What do I want to eat for breakfast? We teach babies early to choose from an abundance of toys.

It took me some time to realize that choosing is an activity that is overvalued in our world and causes much frustration. To me, it is not important whether I buy this product or another; it is more important to maintain my sanity. For important decisions I have come to trust my intuition, my dreams, a *feeling* that I should turn this way rather than that.

We have designed a society that puts choices in our way all the time. We must choose services: a doctor, a lawyer, a plumber. Have you ever moved to a new city and had to choose a doctor at night? Or agonized over how to choose an electrician or a carpenter in an emergency?

How do we choose a profession? What criteria do we use to choose a mate? How do we choose a religion?

Choosing has become the quintessential aspect of Western society. Most other people of this world do not choose often, if at all. Life is what is in front of you.

And what do we do when it comes to new choices, choices our parents never had to make? People have always known how to prevent becoming pregnant, and in this century it has become feasible to choose the number of children you have, but must we now also choose our children's gender? Do we want to abort a fetus that is known to carry the gene for Down's syndrome? Those are choices our parents could not even dream would one day become important decisions. Our forebears would have thought those choices sinful, or presumptuous.

How do we choose who shall live? Modern medical technology can keep a body living long past the point when, ten or twenty years ago, it would have died a natural death. Keeping a body alive, however, with machines and people to service those machines, is expensive. It costs much more than most of us can afford—and often more than insurance companies are willing to reimburse. Do we expect society to pay for machines to keep a body breathing? Society does not have deep pockets anymore. How must it decide who shall continue to breathe and who shall be allowed to die a natural death? Should doctors decide?

There are so many choices, so many alternatives to everything we do, or want, that we have had to learn that sometimes the best choice is not to choose.

We may not want to choose a doctor, or a lawyer, or a plumber, or a new dress, or another career. Perhaps we want to trust luck, or whatever comes our way, or what is available while staying within a budget, or what is available in our neighborhood, or choose only on days that we feel like it.

Because our world has become a world of chaotic over-abundance we feel stressed. The stresses we feel are in large part the result of the overwhelming number of alternatives we must choose from, but also the result of the fact that we have had no time to develop an ethic to help us choose. The headlong rush into new technologies and new ideas, without the time to consider consequences, makes it almost impossible for us to choose. How can we have an opinion about something that did not exist yesterday?

Do we really want experts to choose for us?

We are learning to be leery of expert advice. All too often we find, twenty years later, that the experts were no more expert than we were, that they too were ignorant of the long-term effects of a new drug, a new chemical to control pests, a new way to generate energy. We are beginning to disbelieve experts, distrust authorities and those who claim to know what is best for us.

We call this mad dance *freedom*.

We are proud to be a society of *free* people, by which we mean people who are free to choose, people who, in fact, *must* choose—endlessly, all day—often making choices from alternatives that are so new that we have not had time even to imagine their consequences. We are choosing in a fog.

❊ ❊

Not long ago, most people—almost all people—had few choices they could make.

A million years ago I did not have to choose what I ate. I ate what I could find or catch. I did not have to choose whom I married, or where I lived, or how many children I had.

Even a few hundred years ago—almost everywhere in the world, except perhaps western Europe—I spent my life where I was born, with the people of my tribe. I did what my father did, or perhaps what a maternal uncle did. I married the girl next door, or at most a few doors away. I ate what everyone else ate, most likely what there was available to eat. I wore whatever everyone else wore. I belonged to the religion of my forebears. I died and was buried in the same cemetery where my parents and their parents were buried, or was cremated as they were cremated. I did not have to choose much.

How much simpler life was when we had a bard who sang the songs he knew and we knew as well. How much simpler when there was one healer in our village, and she did not expect *me* to tell her what was wrong because she knew. I did not pay her, although she often expected a gift at midwinter. If the roof leaked, neighbors helped repair it. If the soles of my shoes were worn, the village cobbler repaired them. We ate what was in season. We traded eggs for vegetables, perhaps, or milk for a wool sweater.

Not a bad time, on the whole. A time when a major decision might be whether I should go on a vision quest now or later.

Today we go on a vision quest over the weekend. We take shamanic training at a two-day workshop that is repeated every few weeks for others who want to learn whatever it is that a particular teacher has to say about shamanism. There are a hundred others who will teach us differently about what *they* think shamanism is. There are undoubtedly catalogs that will list the various shamanic traditions we can learn.

Having so many alternatives serves only to devalue all of them.

What has made life in the Western world so stressful is that we think we must choose among a chaos of products and services. Frankly, neither the products nor the services work well anymore—we are in too much of a hurry to give much thought to consequences while we make money, invent new gadgets, start new fads, create new everything. Our very existence on this planet is threatened because, in our haste, we have made—and continue to make—bad choices.

Stress is the price we pay for affluence—an affluence that in the end is little more than a glut of increasingly meaningless choices.

If someone would tell me today to draw something, anything, I too would stare into space with a blank look on my face.

Too many choices.

Bali and the Barong

"What is life?" someone asked me not long ago. I answered, "Jumping from ice floe to ice floe in a raging torrent."

I think of life as a sort of balancing act in an ever-changing environment. If we are fast and agile we can stay upright by jumping to another ice floe just as the one we are standing on is tipping or sliding out from under us. Sometimes we fall into the icy water and we must scramble up another ice floe and go on. And all the while the river is moving who knows where.

The image of the rushing ice floes I thought of myself, but the *idea* I borrowed from the Balinese, whose worldview is that nothing in the world—nothing in the universe—is stable. One can never know what is going to happen next.

In every village in Bali (an island in Indonesia), twice a month, at the full moon and the new moon, an event takes place that Westerners call a dance. The villagers gather in the village square, just before dark. Kids, dogs, and chickens wander here and there. At one end of the village square are two upright stone structures, often elaborately carved, that frame an entrance.

Suddenly a horrible cry is heard, and through this entrance a frightening apparition appears: a screeching old witch in a terrifying mask, breasts made of horizontally striped cotton—bold black alternating with white—hanging to her knees, and a tongue that seems to be on fire hanging between her breasts.

She is Rangda, the chief *leyak,* a witch, but identified with all kinds of misfortune (perhaps related to India's Kali). Sometimes she has one or two helpers adding to the turmoil. In larger villages, these helpers—and their screams—precede her.

The villagers become quieter, but they have seen this often enough. Rangda, who visits twice a month, is a familiar appearance. She strides around the square, threatening, cursing, screaming. She taunts the villagers: "Is there no one then in this blasted village who will defend his home from me?" First one, then more young men (and some not so young) come into the square. They draw their *kris* (daggers with extremely sharp, wavy blades) against Rangda. They will defend the village! They are quite serious about warding off this screaming apparition and the disasters she foreshadows.

Now Rangda stands tall, probably on the steps of the gate, facing the men, pointing all her fingers (gloved with five-inch-long nails that curve down) at them, and it is easy to believe that a force pushes the men back. This almost palpable force ebbs and flows, now allowing the men to come closer to Rangda, then almost literally throwing them back. The villagers seem intensely alive now, observing a battle that is playing out in front of their eyes.

This is real. It is no dance, although it looks choreographed. The force that controls the men is real enough. The villagers watch spellbound—the story may have become routine, but the outcome is always in doubt.

In all of the times that I have seen the Barong, as this event is called, it continues like this: Rangda becomes stronger, so strong in fact that she is able to turn the men's daggers against themselves. They are forced to turn their wrists so that the kris is now aimed at their own chests (bare, of course—Bali is practically on the equator). One can see the point of the kris press but rarely puncture the skin. Yet, these daggers are very sharp.

The men visibly struggle to use all their strength to prevent themselves from being hurt by the kris. They are under great stress, muscles quivering. Sweat is pouring down their faces and bodies. Some say that Rangda puts the men into a trance, which turns their daggers against them, though others say that the only way to survive while resisting Rangda is to put yourself in a trance.

The men are obviously in a deep trance, not the relaxed kind we have learned about in the West. In this trance each of them staggers, bent far backward, holding back the kris that seems to want to pierce the chest of its owner. This is hard work. Later, when it is over, the men are spent. It takes at least a day to recover, I was told.

This goes on for varying lengths of time, until, when the men seem at the end of their endurance, the spirit protector of the village enters: Barong, a wonderful monster, a mythical beast, with a huge carved head. Barong is big; it takes two men to carry the sacred image. The one in front is inside the enormous head, swaying from side to side; the man behind is inside the rest of the elaborate cloth beast.

Barong is a protector. He moves around, reviving men who have fallen. Sometimes, when Rangda is particularly strong, almost all men fall in a faint.

Priests and other helpers offer sips of holy water to those struggling to come out of their trance. Barong does not fight, but he prevents the men from being hurt when they are about to pierce their own chests. He strengthens the men's ability to resist Rangda.

As the men regain some strength and as Rangda loses hers, the battle changes. The few men who can find still more energy chase the witch back through the gate, and the village is safe for another two weeks.

This event takes many hours, sometimes the whole night. It is certainly not entertainment—a trance dance, as some guidebooks call it—but a ceremony. It is all too real. There are times when Rangda wins, when the men cannot prevent her from walking into the village. If that happens, earthquakes shake the ground, volcanoes erupt, epidemics descend, and many other terrible things occur, the Balinese say.

The important fact to remember is that no one ever knows the outcome. A dance is a stylized story, and we often know how it ends. But the ending of a Barong cannot be predicted. Having watched this dance several times, I believe that. It is obviously a battle fought on another plane. It is almost visibly a battle of spirit—good and evil. But that is a Western simplification. The Barong ceremony is not about these two opposing spirits. Rangda is the spiritual force of destruction, Barong is protection, and the people are the spirit of survival, of growth, of life. Twice a month, these forces are testing each other's strengths and weaknesses. It is not so much a dance as it is a trial.

The Barong says something about the Balinese idea of what life is about. To the Balinese the universe, the cosmos (both the physical and the spiritual cosmos, which, to the Balinese, are mirror images) is not neat and orderly. They do not understand the Western idea that says the universe is lawful, that if we know the laws, the cycles, the regularities, then we can predict the future. The Balinese say that the cosmos is unknowable, unpredictable, changing according to no rule or law of man, or even of gods.

That means we must live always and only in the here and now—that is all there is. And we must be prepared, at all times, to move with the changes that are inevitably happening to our world and to us.

Different
Realities

It was my job to travel a few days ahead of the survey team, to prepare the villagers. In Kuala Lumpur, the capital of Malaysia, important people sat down with maps and demographics, and had decided that this village and that would constitute a representative sample of the population. The sample villages also had to be accessible by road, and there had to be a guesthouse nearby—after all, there would be more than twenty people on the survey team, many of them foreigners and important physicians.

I had been assigned this job because I understood what the survey was about and I spoke the language. I was a highly trained (but American-trained) psychologist with anthropological interests, and although I had taken some course work in nutrition, I was not really a nutritionist, nor was I a physician, so obviously I could not do any real work with this survey. But I did speak Malay.

The survey was designed to determine the nutritional status of the population. After interviews had been completed, blood and urine samples taken, laboratory tests run, questionnaires analyzed, food samples chemically broken down and measured, the survey results would provide baseline data on the diet and health status of the population.

For local political reasons, only one ethnic group was to be sampled—the Malays. Two other groups, who together formed a little less than half of the country's population, were not included, perhaps because not all of them had been given the vote when the country received its independence a few years earlier.

An entire planeload of modern scientific equipment and supplies had been sent from the United States. It is true that perhaps as much as half of that would have been available in the country and would have cost much less than what had been paid for shipping. But it had been cheaper, the people who organized these surveys said, to send the whole package, standardized for countries that were then known as developing, which was taken to mean there were no local scientists, physicians, nutritionists, laboratory equipment, and such. Malaysia—rich in many different resources—had an excellent and world-famous nutrition research facility whose studies on dietary deficiencies had become standards for researchers all over the world. Yet, obviously, someone somewhere in the bureaucracy had decided that it was cheaper to send redundant materials—including machines that ran on 120v when the nation's standard was 220v.

The first village was on the east coast, I remember—a community that could have been the locale for a Dorothy Lamour movie. I knew, of course, that I could not just barge in and tell them that they had been chosen (assigned) to be part of a nationwide survey. I must sit down and get to know them or, more important, have them get to know me.

Unfortunately, it did not work that way. My visit had

been planned for a few days only, then on to the next village. The survey would follow closely on my footsteps, keeping to its set schedule; half of the team came from the United States and the individuals in this group could be gone only a few weeks from important positions at home. This was a modern survey, performed with expensive equipment and expensive people; it had to be done by the clock. There was no time for me to be subtle.

The idea of a survey was very strange to the villagers. Since the ten American physicians on the team did not speak the language, they would be assisted by physicians and others from Malaysia who would interpret. The questionnaire was a standard form, I was told, that had been used successfully in many other countries. After the questionnaire, a physician would do a quick physical examination of each of the villagers who had volunteered. In addition, every fifth person would be asked to give a urine sample and every tenth person would be asked to donate some blood.

After meeting the head of the village, I explained the purpose of the survey to the people as best I could. Blood was not something you gave away, the villagers told me. Blood was what kept you alive, after all. Why would anyone want to give blood to a stranger? It was only a small amount, I told them. They shook their heads at yet another example of the incomprehensible foolishness of white people.

Even more strange was the idea of a sample; how could their answers be representative of the whole population of the country? That did not seem possible—after all, were they not unique in this village? They knew quite well that even the people of a neighboring village were *quite* different. However, it was all so strange that they did not question much.

Some people asked, *Give urine and blood for what?* Was there some sort of reward? Would the twenty doctors be able to treat them, perhaps give them medicines, or medical advice?

No, definitely not! I had been instructed to make very clear that the volunteers would not be paid, and they would *not* be given medical advice or treatment—the American physicians who were part of the team were not licensed to practice medicine in Malaysia and the Malaysian physicians would be too busy. We asked the villagers to participate for the sake of science, or, perhaps, to serve their country.

Finally there were no more questions. I knew I had not convinced anybody, but they were too polite to bother me further. They were decent, friendly, helpful people, and they would wait and see what happened, and cooperate as much as they could. This mysterious team that would come to visit might be a diversion.

I talked with many people those two days. I repeated myself, although I tried to come up with different ways to explain what the survey was all about, why it was important for the government to know how healthy people were, why it was important to know if their diets were adequate. I doubt that many people understood the purpose of such an endeavor, but they knew enough not to argue with a white man who arrived in their *kampong* (village) with a government car and a Malay driver. In addition, they were curious. I obviously had some authority; I spoke for the government, so it was probably all right.

The village head told me that, of course, some people would have to work—they would go to the fields or do whatever needed to be done—so those people could not participate, but the people who did not have to work would cooperate. I told myself that it was not my responsibility to worry about the sample.

The team arrived in eighteen Land Rovers. They set up shop in the village community center, a large open space with a floor, a roof, but no walls. Sheets were used to improvise examining rooms.

The leader of the team objected when the children of the village crowded around, looking under the sheets, climbing in trees to look over the sheets, trying to see what was going on. He commanded me to remove the children. I reminded him that if a team of Asians were to come to his hometown, no doubt his children would also be curious.

He looked at me with scorn and declared that, "for damn sure" *his* town would not even let Asians in. "Get those people out of here," he said again.

I could not, of course. I did not try.

Eventually the team got to work without serious interruptions. People stood in long lines, patiently waiting their turn.

✠ ✠

I had the rest of the day off. I was free to wander through the village. It was quiet, with most of the people clustering around the survey site. I talked with some people I had met the day before. Someone offered me a cup of tea. I could relax after the rather harrowing experience of trying to explain what we were going to do.

In the afternoon, the hottest time of the day, when people seek shade somewhere, I found myself sitting on the steps of a house. Somebody mentioned that inside the house there was a very sick woman.

"Yes," the few villagers who stood around affirmed,

nodding knowingly. "She is very sick. She has been sick for many years, and we expect her to die soon."

Without thinking, I asked to go inside. A woman was lying on a mat in a dark corner of the house. There was an air of sickness around her. She was emaciated, but she had an enormously distended abdomen. I am *not* a physician, but I thought that perhaps it was an ovarian cyst.

The woman was barely able to speak, or perhaps she was too shy to talk with a stranger—and a white man at that. I told her she had to go to a hospital as soon as possible; they would make her better. I probably mentioned that at the hospital they might want to operate. She tried to smile. Her children, perhaps eight and ten years old, came in and stood looking at me with big eyes. They did not say anything.

I went outside and said, "Who can talk to this woman? She does not seem to understand. She is very, very sick and needs to go to a hospital right away."

At first there was no response, then a young man spoke up, saying that only her husband—or maybe her brother—could determine whether she should go to a hospital. And although they did not say it in so many words, they implied, with Asian politeness, that it was surely none of *my* business.

"Well, go get the husband then, or the brother, or whomever I need to convince to take her to the hospital." I was not going to give up doing my good deed. Perhaps I felt that by helping this woman I would feel better about being a scout for the survey.

By now there was a small group of people standing outside the house. I told them that I would take her to the hospital in one of our cars.

"Please, find her husband, or her brother, or someone I can talk with."

Later, I realized that I did not *think*. I was on automatic pilot, standing there in my white skin. I do not remember what my feelings were, but I do remember the urgency I felt. Even though all the people said several times that this woman had been sick for a long time and that she was expected to die soon, I felt it was urgent that I take her away from that dark corner in her little house—take her to a modern medical facility, have a surgeon cut out her sickness. I did not think further.

Finally, after what must have been an hour or more, the husband came forward very hesitantly. I explained to him what, of course, he already knew: his wife was very sick. Then I added that she should go to a hospital to get treatment. He listened to me patiently and said he could not really decide that. I had to talk to her brother, or her father.

At this response I grew impatient. "Please, get the brother, then."

There was a little hospital seven miles from the village. The distance would make it difficult for the villagers to take her there, and obviously she could not walk. Since the survey was in the village, one of our vehicles could take her easily enough.

A little later the brother came and an old man who said he was the father of the woman. Again I went through my plea. By now it was obvious that the husband, the brother, and the father of the woman, as well as the growing group of people standing around, were becoming nervous and resentful. In another culture they would have been angry, they would have thrown me out. But Malays are peaceful people who value harmony above all. No one becomes angry because that embarrasses both parties. No one even raises his voice, *ever*.

They obviously did not know how to deal with me, a stranger who had descended on their kampong a few days earlier, followed by twenty doctors in eighteen Land Rovers and a great deal of noise. Perhaps they thought I was the leader of this survey team, rather than an advance scout. I obviously had authority if I could get the use of a vehicle and driver at a snap of my fingers, but it was not an authority they recognized. It all must have been very confusing, I realized much later.

My behavior was particularly confusing because I spoke their language (fluently enough, at the time), and yet did not understand their customs, their *adat* (law). I made demands on them, but I should have known that in the Malay culture no adult ever tells another adult what to do. Anybody who had even a little knowledge of their culture would know that it is simply not done. It is rude, crude, contemptible behavior to tell another what to do. Even raising your voice is an offense in the Malay culture.

I am ashamed to admit that I probably never considered what the woman herself might be thinking and feeling while we argued about her, without her present.

In the end it must have been my inexplicable insistence that made the father, the brother, and the husband agree to have the woman moved from her house and taken to the hospital. One of the vehicles had once served as an ambulance; it carried a stretcher of sorts. We loaded the woman on the stretcher and put her in the car amid an ominous silence in the now fairly large group of people.

At the hospital they took one look at her and said she could not be admitted without five pints of blood—hospital policy. If the blood were not donated before admission, they would never get it later, they said. I knew that to be true.

It was past four in the afternoon. I convinced the staff to keep the woman in the waiting room while I rushed back to the village to get able-bodied men to come back with me to donate blood. Not only had I forced my will on the whole village, now I had come back to beg five people to give blood.

I was obsessed. I talked, I ranted, I cajoled—and finally I bribed five men to come with me. I paid them for working time lost, even though it was late, well past the time when anyone would work. I could not stop myself.

We arrived at the hospital as it was getting dark. The men gave blood, I paid them, and the vehicle took them back to the village.

Near that village there was a guesthouse where some of us were staying. (Guesthouses were a relic of colonial times, usually bungalows available to important travelers, which meant, originally, white people.) The woman was in the hospital. I was exhausted, but felt a sense of accomplishment. I do not believe I thought in terms of saving her life, but I definitely felt pleased. I had won, and probably I imagined that I had done what every normal (white) person would have done. The doctor at the hospital had confirmed my guess—she did have an ovarian cyst. They would remove it surgically early the next morning.

I felt good.

�֍   ✖֍

It was dark, perhaps seven o'clock in the evening. I was sitting on the veranda, my feet up. A woman approached and stood on the grass on the other side of the railing. She asked me if I was the man who had taken her sister to the hospital.

I repeated what had become a sort of refrain: "Your sister is very sick and needs to be in a hospital."

I did not get a chance to say much more than that.

She began talking and continued for what must have been at least half an hour. She never raised her voice, but she made *very* clear how upset she was. She did not move. She never took her eyes off my face.

"Do you know what you have done?" she said. "Sister is very sick. She has been sick for five years—we all expect her to die. Sister knows she is going to die. Her husband knows she is going to die. Her children know she is going to die. I know. The whole kampong knows she is going to die. We have all had time to accept that. We grieve for her; we grieve with her husband and children. We feel her pain. She has much pain, but she is a brave woman and she does not complain. We take care of her as best we can. All the people of the kampong help with the children. We cook for them. We bring them the best of what we have. We sit with her, day and night. We pray with her. We know her sickness; it is our sickness as well. The sickness has been with us a long time."

She paused to take a deep breath, and went on.

"Now you come. You rip her out of her home, out of the village. You cause so much commotion that we do not know anymore what is happening." Again she took a deep breath. "Maybe this is the end of the world . . ."

She paused only briefly, to go on almost immediately. "What right do you have to take her away from husband, children, the kampong? She is sick—she needs us, all of us, around her. Now she is all alone with strangers. She should be with her family, her friends in her kampong. Instead she is in this stone building, with nobody to give her the food she likes. She is all alone in a cold room. I know; I went to see her and was told I could not. I am her sister. I have taken care of her for five years!

"Of course we know she is sick. She has been sick all these years. We, all of us, the whole kampong, have adjusted ourselves to her condition. She herself has resigned herself to her condition. The children have adjusted themselves to the fact that their mother is dying. She was sick long before you ever showed up with your cars and all those people in white coats.

"That sickness is part of our daily life. We all live with it. She herself is ready to die. She knows she is dying. She is not afraid; she is a good woman. We all know she is going to die, and when she dies, the kampong will die a little. She is the kampong, the kampong is she. We all die a little when she dies."

She paused and looked away. "When she dies, we will bury her and life will go on as before. Her death will be a gentle leave-taking, not this rude tearing away—not like you taking my sister away to hospital!"

She stumbled over the words; she was angry, but could not show that.

"Do you know what is going to happen when she dies now, in hospital, so far away from home? Do you know what is going to happen when she dies there?" She was crying softly. "We cannot even bury her. Our religion forbids moving the body more than an hour [an hour's walk]. If she had died at home we would have buried her in the little cemetery of the kampong. We could have come to visit her grave whenever we wanted. If she dies now, she will be buried with strangers, sick people, at a cemetery near hospital, and we cannot visit her often—it is too far to walk. Did you think about that?"

Again she paused to take a deep breath. "Who do you

think you are, anyway? Tuan Allah, the Lord God himself, that you can show up in our kampong and disturb the flow of our lives? Do you have any right to take one of us—a sister from the same mother who bore me—out of our lives? Do you have any right to throw us all in a panic? How can you do that? Yes, my sister is dying. We are all together in this sickness. All of us are dying a little with her. Now what? What are we to do now? Tell me that. What are we to do?"

She shamed me, more perhaps than anybody had shamed me before. I felt myself shrinking. Whatever satisfaction I had felt doing a "good deed" that day evaporated. Instead, I experienced my own ruthless arrogance, my insensitivity to people who were so much like the warm, wonderful people I had grown up with. How could I have forgotten?

I had done what was proper and expected in my own world, perhaps, in my own reality. But this was not my reality. The reality of the villagers was different—and I knew that. I knew their world; I had lived in their world.

I was mortified to realize that I had forgotten not only my manners, but also my sensitivity. I could not answer this woman—what could I say, anyway?

She was right.

During her monologue I had noticed a few people watching from far away. I understood that they were staying away to spare us the added embarrassment of an audience. In this culture, I remembered, one never, ever, embarrasses someone else. This woman, in shaming me, was embarrassing me, but also embarrassing herself. I knew what it must have cost her to say what she did.

With a visible effort she collected herself, and said,

"How much chance has sister, now that she is in hospital?"

The word for hospital in Malay is *rumah sakit,* "house of sickness" or "house for the sick." The way she spit out the word, I knew she felt strongly that the place where her sister had gone was truly a house of vile, ugly sicknesses, not at all like the world of the kampong, where the woman's sickness was a natural part of life and death. Her sister, part of the kampong, was far away in a stone building constructed especially to hold people who had many different kinds of illness, in a place where they cut people open, a building that smelled strange, run by people who would not allow her own sister to see her. This building was alien, unnatural.

I had called the doctor about half an hour earlier. He had told me that the planned surgery would be touch and go. The woman would have a fifty-fifty chance of making it, he said.

I told her sister, "Half and half."

She almost spat on the grass. "Half a chance that she will die, half a chance that she will live? Is that any better than she had before?"

✠ ✠

Months later I heard that the woman lived to be discharged from the hospital. Whether she recovered fully, I do not know. I was too ashamed to go back.

Succession

When I studied dietary behavior in Malaysia, it soon became evident that it was not enough to ask what people ate, or did not eat. I also had to know how they lived, what their daily lives were like. How many meals did they eat each day? Who cooked? Did a family sit around a table? Did they even sit down at all to eat together? The answers to these questions are very different from what one would expect in a Western setting. Malays often eat only two meals a day, not three; the family does not sit around a table—they sit on the floor; and very often people eat when they are hungry, not together at a specified mealtime.

I learned early that we cannot assume that others do what people do in America, or that they do it in the same way. Cross-cultural research cannot be broken down into small pieces. In order to find out what the typical diet is for any group of people, we must also know something about how these people live, what is available to them, what is important in their culture. For all these reasons, it was obvious that I should spend time in Malay villages, just observing, hanging out with people, getting to know them.

I had the use of a car and driver from the institute where

I worked. The first time we visited a village, it turned out that the driver had distant relatives there, which made my being there more natural. I could explain my presence by saying that I accompanied the driver when he went to see his relatives and friends. We returned to that village twice a week for the next year and a half.

It was probably on the first visit that I was introduced to the village chief, or the "head" of the kampong, as he is called in Malay. He was an elderly gentleman, very dignified, who did not say much. He and others accepted my presence with equanimity and very little curiosity. I explained that I studied the diets of people, but that I was in their village simply to familiarize myself with their daily lives. They seemed to accept that without much question. The driver's first wife was from the village, and so he was still considered part of the kampong. After a few visits I knew most of the people by sight, and many of them by name.

Then, one day, the village head died.

I was curious how a new head would be appointed or elected. Was headship in a Malay village hereditary? The anthropological literature about the local form of government was vague and confusing. Some anthropologists had described a very authoritarian system—after all, there are sultans in Malaysia who are absolute rulers, which does not sound democratic to American scientists. Others said that chiefship (headship) was hereditary, that a son follows his father. Most agreed that the head is male, but at least one anthropologist talking about village life fifty or so years ago mentioned a female chief.

The process was certainly leisurely. Nobody seemed in a hurry to find or get a new head. In fact, they were without a head for over a year and a half—not unusual, I learned later—but the villagers did not seem much concerned.

I knew that the district commissioner appoints heads of villages, but I did not know what criteria he would use to make his appointment, nor did the district commissioner seem to be in a hurry to carry out this duty. When I asked people in the village how the district commissioner would choose a new head, people smiled and did not answer.

On my twice-weekly visits I would wander through the village, chat with friends, listen to news of births and deaths and the harvest, and I would end up at the place where some of the older men and some women would sit around, aimlessly talking.

In the early afternoon, when white people take a nap, Malays hang around, very quietly. Sometimes someone will say a word or two, and after a while someone else might answer. It was not really a conversation—it felt more like friends being together, feeling very comfortable with each other.

After the death of the village head there were fleeting comments about what a nice person he had been, or someone would mention a particular quality he had: he was such a patient person, he never became angry, he was good to his wife, his children had done well.

Later, I called this Phase One of the process of finding a new village head, or having one appointed, a process that lasted perhaps six months.

Gradually, almost without my being aware at first that these random comments were changing, someone would say something about what the new village head might be like, or what qualities would be important in a new head. They would often joke lightly, laugh, say things like, "Oh, I would rather have a village head who knows how to deal with the outside world," or, "Maybe the new village head should be a young person." Later I decided this must be Phase Two, lasting a few months.

I had made notes on my visits and when I read over what I had recorded a month or so earlier, to my surprise I found that vague remarks were getting more specific. I noticed, for instance, that more and more comments were made about specific problems the village had. One of those problems was that the ditches that used to carry off the rainwater had become filled with silt. A few times there had been near floodlike conditions. Or a few people mentioned how hard it was to get to the other side of the river because the bridge that had been there had washed away some years ago. They all knew how to rebuild the bridge, but who would start such a project?

Aha! I thought. *They are looking for a village head with leadership qualities.* In my mind I almost decided that this would be Phase Three, and I expected that now, finally, they would come to some sort of conclusion, a decision. Yet I knew that Malays approach decision making in very round-about ways. Their language does not lend itself to being specific. It is a language of indirection. Until the modern age there was no word for *I*. The word that is used now originally meant "your humble servant," or "your slave."

Simple Malay and Indonesian have no tenses; the context of a sentence determines whether a statement is meant to refer to present, past, or future (rarely the future). But more than anything else, it is a language of poetry, of hints at meaning rather than exactness, of allusions rather than pointed information.

So when I thought further about the turn these random remarks were taking, it seemed unlikely that they would lead to what I thought of as a resolution to the problem of getting or finding a new head. I must mention, again, that I never heard anything to suggest that *not* having a village head was a problem for anyone except myself.

One of the basic tenets of Malay culture is that nobody tells anybody what to do. Adults never order a child older than about two to do something or not to do something. The language does not allow for such commands. There is a classic and true story about the Western physician who tells a mother, "Your child should have a shot." The mother turns to her three-year-old, and asks the child whether he wants a shot. When the child says no, there is no argument. A Western doctor or even a Western-trained Malay doctor does not quite know what to do in such a situation.

So leadership in that culture cannot mean what it means in our culture. Even a village head could not possibly tell people what to do, I knew.

After a few more months passed, I noticed that the comments began to become more personal. Someone would say, for instance, "Well, Mohammad knows about building bridges," or, "Isan is a very patient man." Nobody would propose a specific person, but more than a year after the death of the old head, names were being tossed out to evaporate in that typical, vague Malay way of not saying anything, but hinting at something.

I gave up analyzing the process and organizing it in phases. I saw that what was happening was a natural flow of thoughts, ideas, and words that were never expressed— that could not be expressed. This was not an election, and I assumed that at some point, when he got around to it, the district commissioner would pick a name out of a hat.

Then a visitor came to the village and hung around, much as I did. He was there several times when I was there, perhaps for a period of a month or more. He was a nice, kindly, older gentleman, who, it was said, was a friend or relative of the district commissioner. The visitor rarely said anything (neither did I, naturally). He listened, as did I.

To a Westerner all this vague talk was frustratingly unspecific, never coming to the point. Of course that *was* the point of these ruminations. In Malay culture the worst sin is to embarrass someone, so you never talk directly to someone, you do not really look him or her in the eye, you do not raise your voice, you always couch your comments in the most unspecific, general terms. As much as possible, you talk in allusions.

Then, one day, for no reason that I could imagine, the district commissioner appointed a cousin of the late village head to be the new head—a *distant* cousin, the driver told me with much emphasis. He himself was also a distant cousin.

The appointed cousin had been mentioned frequently in those hanging-out sessions, but so had at least half the people of the village. I knew him well, by now. He was a quiet, unassuming person, honest, soft-spoken, obviously intelligent, someone who thought before he said anything but then usually seemed to say just the right thing. He was probably in his middle to late thirties, married, and the father of two small children. Both he and his wife were healthy, not too poor—though it is almost impossible for an outsider to know whether someone is poor or rich in a Malay village because nobody wants to stand out or be different. Even the richest man will live as his neighbors do, without ostentation, and never with conspicuous consumption. The appointed man was considered handsome; his face was not scarred. He had always behaved with decorum, as far as I knew. He was a model citizen, it seemed. The villagers seemed happy. The new head was obviously well respected.

After the installation ceremonies were over, I tried to figure out what the appointment had been based on. While the new village head was related to the late head, the son of the old head had been overlooked. As far as I knew, the chosen cousin was no expert bridge builder, and he knew no more about drainage ditches than anyone else. (Everyone in the village knew where the old ditches had been, and sometime later, when they finally got around to it, it was easy to reconstruct them.) Certainly there had not been an election, as we understand the term. The whole process had seemed almost arbitrary to me, although it was obviously what people had expected to happen. The appointed cousin did not appear to have what we would call leadership qualities; he was an unassertive person—but then, no traditional Malay is assertive. When I asked people why he had been appointed, they shrugged, "Mr. District Commissioner . . ."

As soon as I said it, I knew it had been the wrong question to ask. I had asked an embarrassing question—a direct question that must be answered, or at least was more difficult to ignore. By asking it I had put them on the spot.

I waited a week or so, then asked, "What are the qualifications for head of a village?"

The village head has to be the face of the village, I was told.

I was not quite sure what that meant, but an explanation came soon after. At the time, the government was establishing health clinics in many parts of the country, and they had chosen a small town six miles from the village as the location to serve this and other nearby villages. Of course, walking six miles there and six miles back with a sick child is a day's work when few people have bicycles and there is no bus service. The clinics may have been considered to be nearby by white people and the few people in the cities who had cars, but they were far away for the people who were expected to use them.

When the clinic held its formal opening, the new village head attended with his wife and their two children. They walked. It was then that I saw what the villagers meant when they said that a village head has to be the face of the village. The head of the village was dignified, with definite personality. He dressed in traditional costume, but he wore shoes. He spoke softly, but clearly and well. He made an effort to talk with the foreigners present. He certainly made the village look good.

✳ ✳

Thirty years ago Malay villages did not have a government as we understand it. There was no police to enforce laws. Their only law was the adat, a set of customs and traditions—the essence of Malay culture. The adat cannot be added to; it is not like our man-made laws. The head of a village was not expected to assert leadership—he could not organize what should be done, he could not delegate authority to others. He was a figurehead, the face representing the village to the outside world. But he was also the face that villagers could and did rally around, the embodiment of the identity of their kampong. I suspect it is not too different today. It is a system that works well enough.

The newly elected head was related to the last head, but not in a direct line. He was appointed, but appointed after a long and leisurely process that gave all the villagers a voice—and yet it was not an election.

It makes me wonder: Is that how we too did things in our villages?

Dimensions of Healing

In our society—in our reality—when you are sick, you go to a doctor. Perhaps you go to the emergency ward of a nearby hospital if you have no health insurance, but you still call it going-to-the-doctor. In fact, the phrase is so familiar that it almost has become a single word.

There are assumptions and meanings attached to going-to-the-doctor. For instance, there is a sort of holy assumption that we *choose* a doctor. We also talk as if we each have our own doctor. We know, of course, that neither of those assumptions is true. We do not really choose; we see whomever we can afford, or whoever is conveniently nearby, or the doctor our health plan allows us to see. Few of us have our own doctor anymore, although forty or fifty years ago at least middle-class people had a family doctor. Forty years ago doctors also made house calls.

In many parts of the world, when you are sick you go to a healer. These healers have different names in different cultures, but they have in common the age-old belief that *healing* is an intrinsic capacity of human beings. When you look behind the ceremony, the dress, the ritual, what all native healers do is take away barriers to healing, or strengthen what we would now call the patient's immune system.

Not long ago we looked upon health and illness in much the same way as these native healers. I grew up before miracle drugs. As a child we learned how important it was to wash all wounds thoroughly with soap and water; using any kind of soap and almost any kind of water was better than leaving dirt in a wound. Washing could be painful, but it was impressed on us that it was necessary. We had hydrogen peroxide to clean wounds, which was wonderful for scrapes and shallow cuts because the bubbles added a sort of mechanical cleaning action. We had iodine that stained and stung, although it was many years before I learned that it is the alcohol that stings, not the iodine. Not having miracle drugs also meant that prevention was more important than treatment. It meant, probably, that more people relied on what we now call the immune system. We grew up with the idea that the healthier we were overall, the less chance we would have of getting sick.

It was not unusual then for non-Western healers to work side by side with Western-trained doctors. Different kinds of doctors might use different approaches, but no kind of healing was better than another. I knew that both Western and non-Western doctors were healers. And I knew that I, too, wanted to be a healer.

That meant, I thought, that I must study medicine. My timing was bad, however. I began medical school in Holland, two weeks before World War II started, and a few months later we were occupied by Germans troops. I was able to finish the first part of medical studies (the clinical subjects), but I had barely started the second part, beginning with gross anatomy, when I discovered I was allergic to the formaldehyde used to preserve cadavers, so could not continue my studies. In a strange twist of synchronicity, at about that time the Germans decided universities were hotbeds of resistance. All universities were closed and did not open again until the Allied Forces ended the war, three years later.

When the universities opened again, I changed direction and decided to study psychology. Even though eventually I earned two degrees in psychology (neither in clinical psychology), I never lost my consuming interest in healing.

The more I learned of the Western medical establishment (as a patient and as a student of medical systems), the more I realized that our system of medicine is not designed for healing. Doctors and patients alike are so overawed by the miracles of modern chemistry that we forget who healers were and what they did before penicillin. Both doctors and patients believe that healing comes from drugs, from outside intervention, forgetting that until recently healing was always what the body did, perhaps aided or stimulated by a healer.

Modern (by this I mean technological) medicine has swept the world in recent years, although some years ago there were still a few areas where native healers plied their trade. It is true that in some parts of the world—including the United States—what we call alternative medicine continues to be practiced. Western doctors and Western-trained doctors, however, have become the norm almost everywhere. It was in the twentieth century that medicine replaced healing. Certainly people live longer today, which means the world has more people. The increase in population, however, started long before the last century, and is almost certainly the consequence of better health, better food, better sanitation, and better water, rather than better medicine.

✲ ✲

The emphasis on medical technology has meant the delivery of two messages. One is that the human body is like a machine and far too complex for a layperson to understand, let alone control. We are not supposed to have much knowledge of what goes on inside our bodies. There are an endless number of specialists who know best.

The other message is that modern medicine does best with extreme conditions. The greater part of the time, energy, and money of the medical system is invested in ever more daring and technologically brilliant techniques for prolonging the life of people who, even a few years ago, would have been allowed to die.

✸　✸

When my family and I lived in Malaysia, there were doctors trained in Western medicine, but there also were traditional healers.

Malays in Malaysia were certainly not primitive; they were citizens of a modern state who drove cars over excellent roads, and who had radio and television. Yet many Malays chose to stay in their kampongs, their native environment. Their culture did not fare well in cities. The Malay culture is remarkably coherent.

In our world we imagine that the unit of society is the family, but in Malay culture the unit of society is the kampong. It is the family to which a person belongs. More than from blood relationships, a person's identity comes from the kampong.

As is everything, this too is changing. The family is no longer the building block of our society (if it ever was). In other cultures, traditional relationships are disintegrating in the mad rush to modernization, urbanization, and because of the enormous increase in numbers of people. In Malaysia there was a *bomoh* (native healing practitioner) in most kampongs. I came to know several of these men and one woman (though female bomohs were not rare, I knew only one of them).

A bomoh would tell you that he or she was an ordinary person, just like anyone else. One of the very strong values of Malay culture was egalitarianism; at least outwardly, people seemed the same—a rich man did not live in a bigger or showier house than a poor man, and if he had a car, he would park it outside the kampong. The bomoh, too, lived in a house just like any other.

When consulting a bomoh, a sick person would come to his house. The patient would wait outside until noticed. The bomoh, naturally, would know the patient—after all, they were neighbors. He would sit down in front of the house, or perhaps on the little porch, next to the patient or beside the mother or father holding a sick child. They would chat for a few minutes about the family, about what is happening in the kampong. And then, very gently, almost imperceptibly, the bomoh would move to sit in front of the patient. The bomoh would probably hold a sick child in his lap. While he continued to talk, he would gently touch the patient in the neck, to feel for a fever, to feel the pulse, to feel for muscle tone. He would look at the hair (damp or dry, lustrous or dull), the fingers, and the nails. He would gently feel a swollen stomach, swollen joints. The bomoh would not go through a list of symptoms, but gradually, in an easy conversation with the parent or the patient, he would learn what the problem was, when it started, and how or where, if that was relevant.

The bomoh did a fairly thorough examination and conducted an intake interview, but without instruments—no

thermometers, blood pressure cuffs, tongue depressors—
and without pay or records.

In contrast, when my children went to a Western-
trained doctor, they were put on a flat table under a glaring light, and were held down, sometimes forcibly, by
parents and nurses, while the doctor, in a white coat, prod-
ded and poked. The child's body was an object brought to
be fixed. Little or no friendly talk passed between medical
personnel and patient. Western-trained doctors are professionals, which can mean distant. In this country the distance is further expressed in the custom of calling patients
by their first name, while the patient, of course, addresses
the physician as "Doctor." A bomoh was never addressed as
"Bomoh." Everyone knew him or her by name.

Some bomohs will give their patients Western drugs—at
that time all medicines were available without a prescrip-
tion in Malaysia. Bomohs would carefully read the fine
print on the inserts included in the packages of medication
to understand the possible side effects and drug interac-
tions before they would hand them to a patient. When I
asked one bomoh why he used Western medicines, he
looked quite surprised and said, "Why not? They work."

I knew some bomohs who would give antibiotics, but
they would personally hand the patient one dose, with
water and perhaps a cracker or some rice, and then tell the
patient (or parent) to come back in the evening before sunset, when they would give another dose. The following
morning the patient would arrive for the first dose of that
day, along with some rice, and so it would go until the cycle
of medication had been completed.

A few of the bomohs I knew did not object to sending
a patient to a Western clinic or hospital, if that seemed

necessary. Bomohs are intelligent people. Those I knew studied to keep up with what was going on in the world, but always remained warm, caring people who practiced a noninvasive, personal, and informal method of healing— no rubber gloves or white uniforms, no paperwork, no office, no standard procedures.

Though many of the government's medical clinics were located far away from the kampongs, in small cities or towns where electricity and reliable water were available and where supplies could be brought in by car, the doctors did not seem to understand why so few Malays attended the clinic. When one physician asked me my thoughts on the reason for this, I asked him to come with me to his waiting room (he had never set foot in his own waiting room before).

The clinic building was concrete (which becomes *hot* in the tropics). The waiting room was narrow—benches lined the long sides of the room—and poorly ventilated. Because the air was close, I knew the patients felt that it was a "sick" environment; they feared contamination from other people's illness.

A nurse directed operations from a small window at the end of the room. The nurse was Chinese—very few Malays at that time were health professionals—and she would yell loudly. Though she did this to be heard, perhaps, speaking loudly in the Malay culture is a sign of being crude.

"NEXT!" the nurse would call out—and people would have to come to the window with a sick child who was tired, hot, and very uncomfortable. Without looking at either the child or the parent, the nurse would write in a book while she went down the list of questions for her intake interview: "Name of patient, birth date?" (*I do not know; I am not sure.*) "Name of mother, name of father, where do you live?" she asked next. Then, "What is wrong with the child?"*(I do not know.)* "Well then, why are you here?"

Patients knew only that the bomoh did not ask what was wrong—he was supposed to know that. Or he would find out soon enough during his gentle chat, without having to ask outright. By the time the nurse had filled out the forms, the parent was confused and intimidated, the child in tears.

After this interview the patient was sent to the examining room, an even more frightening experience, where glaring lights blinded, where people dressed all in white (the color of mourning) wore masks to make them more impersonal. Doctors and nurses wore rubber gloves—which patients interpreted to mean who these doctors did not even want to touch the people who came to see them.

After the examination, mother and child would come back into the waiting room, the nurse would reach into a bottle, grab a handful of pills, and say, "Here, give the child one of these pills four times a day, with some water, before a meal." Finally, to add insult to injury, the nurse would stick out her hand and ask for money!

A bomoh does not get paid. He is a neighbor who helps because he is a friend. When the child has recovered, the mother may bring him a nice chicken, a piece of cloth, or some special fruit that is in season—but that is not considered payment.

In the clinic the nurse would yell again, "NEXT!"—and the sick child, asleep now, would be carried by the mother many miles, on foot, home to the kampong.

✠   ✠

In order to organize society, we create institutions, we build buildings, we train millions of people to perform very specialized activities. We make endless forms to record and report what we are doing. We create armies of people to supervise other people, and of course the supervisors themselves have to be supervised as well.

These systems acquire a life of their own. We seem to forget that they were created around an idea. All systems (health systems, economic systems, or political systems) are creations of our unique way of looking at the world, our reality. Systems are expressions of our beliefs.

We have created an enormous healthcare system, for example, that in today's society provides at least 10 percent of all jobs, circulates an enormous amount of money, and utilizes thousands of buildings, clinics, hospitals, and laboratories. It incorporates the latest in medical science and technology, but it is rooted in our unique beliefs about health and illness, life and death.

In today's reality, for instance, *life* has come to mean the life of an individual. We believe death is something to be conquered, defeated, denied as long as possible. Some doctors feel that when a patient dies, they have "lost the fight." We believe people of all ages, regardless of prognosis, and regardless of what some call their quality of life, should be kept breathing as long as possible. To do that, a disproportionate amount of money, technology, and time is devoted to mechanically prolonging the breathing of terminally ill people. We spend much more time, money, and energy on keeping a few people alive than on helping to keep all people healthier. Our belief that being alive is the ultimate and supreme value might be more understandable if there were only a few humans left—but there are six billion of us, and tomorrow there will be seven and then eight billion!

All our systems are designed around a belief that everything is so complex and difficult to manage that we require experts to help us navigate. There are experts for every aspect of life. Everyone who does anything at all needs training, probably a degree or a diploma, certainly a license. The result is that each of us is powerless, except in the narrow slice of the world we ourselves inhabit. There is hardly anything we can—or are allowed to—do for ourselves. We are made to think that we must ask for expert advice for everything we do.

Because systems are rooted in beliefs, we and even the experts find it difficult to imagine that there might be other ways of doing things. We cannot imagine that there are other beliefs. Thus we think that ours is the only true reality, that other people, other cultures, are backward, archaic, underdeveloped, and so on.

By judging others as less than ourselves, we cannot learn from them. That is sad, because we throw away, suppress, and deny the accumulated wisdom of generations of ancestors.

✸   ✸

Each culture has its own thoughts about disease. In some cultures sickness or disease is thought to be punishment from the gods. In others being sick is something like permission to take a break—a legitimate reason to take a day off. Some cultures believe that sickness is a disturbance of energies. Chinese medicine, probably the oldest surviving system of healing in the world, is based on the observation that our bodies are interrelating energy fields that can—and often need to be—adjusted or stimulated in order that we may be whole again. Herbs, diets, and acupuncture (and exercises like tai chi), in the Chinese way of thinking, all help to balance, adjust, or stimulate the many energies in and around our bodies.

In the West we believe that illness is the result of an assault, an attack from outside the body, usually by microorganisms. That means patients are victims, and medical scientists are forced to think in terms of which organism causes which disease. The question, of course, determines the answer; sooner or later we always find new organisms that "cause" a new disease. But we miss much important information because we do not ask questions that are regularly asked in other cultures, such as why one particular patient acquires a disease that is transmitted through the air while another, breathing the same air, does not. Nor have we asked, until recently, how we might strengthen someone's immune system—perhaps the most common question non-Western healers ask themselves.

Malays believe that the cause of any sickness is disharmony. The particular form the disease takes may be the result of an invasion of some microorganism, but why this person becomes ill while the next person does not is a consequence of the kind and degree of disharmony in the patient's internal and external environment. Malays and others have known about the immune system all along, although they do not call it that.

Healing for Malays is, above all, about restoring harmony. In a very real sense all of Malay culture is focused on maintaining harmony among people and between people and their environment. Malay culture teaches the great value of not rocking the boat, of making gentle movements and not offending or even embarrassing others, of walking carefully and speaking softly. Where there is disharmony, it is often the healer who helps to restore harmony, although to facilitate this, as a bomoh explained to me, the healer may give a patient herbs to help him cope with symptoms.

Ultimately, however, the effort of both healer and patient must be to restore balance to the patient's environment, both physical and social.

The aborigines in Malaysia, I learned, think of illness in yet another way. To them sickness is a signal, a warning: *Hey, you are doing something wrong! Stop and change!* Healing for them means first finding out what is wrong so that it can be changed or righted. The wrong may not be a behavior; it may be a thought, a feeling, or even a word. It is easier to change a behavior than it is to take back a thought, but it must be done to get well.

Healing for the aborigines is almost wholly in the hands of the sick person. If you are ill, you alone can heal yourself—no one can do it for you. What an outsider can do is find out what is wrong, diagnose the illness—and perhaps open the way for healing energy to enter the patient. As I came to know the aborigines better, I found that there were people who assisted in the process of finding out what was behind the illness and making what we would call a diagnosis. The same people would also open the way, or pass healing strength to the sufferer.

I talked with a few of these aboriginal healers, who sometimes called themselves bomoh (but that was for my sake, I am sure—they knew I was studying Malay bomohs). Their role in the process of healing was different from the role of a Malay bomoh. In terms of what they did, they seemed more like counselors, perhaps.

We tend to think that assisting another in healing must be a profession, because we think in terms of experts and professionals. The aborigines do not. They have no experts and, as in most simple societies, there are no professionals.

The names they gave me for what they were doing varied. The name they had for themselves did not indicate what they did, but only suggested who they were. I called them healers; that is not what they called themselves.

The aborigines were consistently and deliberately simple people. What the healer did was simple: he or she talked with the person who hurt. These talks were not supplications, not requests for healing. They may have been addressed to spirits, or to other unseen forces, but ultimately they were discussions with the energies around the sickness.

It was possible for the healer to do this work when the patient was not present. A hollow bamboo tube was then used, closed on one side so that it could hold water, sometimes decorated with traditional designs. Water was poured into the bamboo container, and a coin or something that had been close to the person with pain was placed in the water. The bamboo tube then stood in for the patient.

After the healer had determined what was wrong, healing energy was passed to the water (to the coin, which then gave it to the water). When the patient drank the water, he was able to heal himself. I asked whether the sufferer would learn what is wrong from the water. I was assured that, yes, the message—which tells what is wrong—would pass to the sufferer.

The water healing was colorful and seemed "ethnic," but I had the impression that, in fact, it was far more common for the sufferer and the healer to perform the healing ritual together.

One aborigine healing session I attended went like this: First the healer asked the *ati* of the sick person to make clear to the patient what she should do to remove the stiffness in her shoulder (which was considerably swollen, bruised, and seemingly immobile). *Ati* (or *hati,* with a silent *h*) literally means "liver," but is used also to mean "heart" or "emotions"; in context here it was obviously used for what we would call "soul." Then the healer went through a whole list of possibilities: maybe the woman was angry at that arm (being angry or aggressive is tabu, the worst emotion a Sng'oi can express), or maybe she had just worked too hard digging roots. Perhaps someone bumped against that shoulder when she was carrying something on her head, and to keep what she was carrying from falling down she moved the shoulder in a wrong way.

While the healer was going down the list, he rubbed the woman's shoulder, lightly at first, then a little more firmly. I was watching the woman's expression. She was obviously in pain. But as the healer, in a singsong, droning voice, continued his listing of possibilities, he suggested, "Maybe you fell down and you broke your fall with your arm."

Before he could finish his sentence, the woman opened her eyes and looked up, surprised, as if to say, "Yes, of course that was it!"

The healer continued to rub her shoulder, but now he was kneading, to soften the tissues, as he explained to me in an aside, "So that the healing can know where to enter her shoulder."

The woman remembered, "Yes, I fell down on the way to the water. I slipped and fell on that shoulder." She turned her head and pointed with her chin to the hurt shoulder. "I was carrying a child and did not want the child to be hurt, so the shoulder sort of buckled under me—" and as she said this, she let out a scream as if reliving the fall.

She began to turn her lower arm inward, elbow out, while holding onto the immobilized hand with the other, healthy one. The healer at the same time put more pressure on the back of the shoulder until something moved. Again the woman screamed, but this time more softly than before. She tried to move the arm, but it remained immobile. Then she smiled and said, "I still cannot move it, but I know that tomorrow I will be fine—I feel the healing working."

The next day the shoulder was less swollen, and she could move her arm a little. Patient and healer had worked together to effect a return to normal. Yet the patient clearly felt that *she* had done the actual healing, that the role of the healer had been to show her what had brought about her trauma and to pass along healing energy.

On another occasion I asked a healer whether sickness can sometimes be caused by spirits, by bad energies from outside. A doctor had told me—with considerable irritation in his voice—that aborigines considered tuberculosis a sickness of spirits. At the time tuberculosis had become a serious health problem. It occurred to me that spirits as a cause are much the same as invading microorganisms (in this case, tubercle bacilli).

The healer looked at me, thought for a minute, then said, "Sickness is inside, but sometimes we forget to take care of ourselves."

"And then what happens?" I asked.

He paused, then said, "The coughing sickness is not our sickness; we never had the coughing sickness before. Maybe soldiers brought it, or your people did." Then he frowned.

He was right. Tuberculosis is one of the diseases that accompany the spread of civilization. It is we, the civilized, who bring diseases like tuberculosis, syphilis, smallpox, and even the common cold, along with other bacterial and viral diseases, to people who lived in isolation and did not have an opportunity to acquire immunities.

I pressed him: "Does that mean there is nothing you can do about the coughing sickness?"

Again he thought. "That is right, there is nothing we can do. Maybe as we get used to it, we can be healthy again." He was silent for a long time. Then, as an afterthought, he said, "But I do not think so. I think we will die."

He looked at me then with an expression that I can only describe as sly when he added another word, in Malay: *"Naik..."*

What he said seemed very strange and out of context. Literally, *naik* means "climb," "rise out of," or "emerge." Perhaps he meant, "leave our bodies"? He would not explain when I asked him what he meant.

I thought he meant, *We are dying out ... climbing out* of the shadow world, as the aborigines call the world we live in.

Toward the end of my stay in Malaysia a dedicated young English doctor created a health system designed for aborigines. A hospital was established in the jungle on the outskirts of the capital, Kuala Lumpur, thought to be a familiar environment but also accessible by road. Aborigine settlements were given battery-operated radios to summon medical help when needed, and people were trained to use this equipment. Finally, helicopters stood by to transport patients.

The hospital was not run like a Western hospital. Neither the patients nor the medical staff wore uniforms, and patients were admitted with their families, who could prepare customary food for the patients. The treatment was with Western drugs—which was the best way to treat a sickness that they recognized as not theirs.

✠　✠

In our world we applaud medical intervention that saves a life. We spend endless resources to extend the life span of an individual for a day, a week, a year.

We may think that our resources are the rewards of our efforts, our productivity, but in the earth's closed ecosystem when we use resources (trees, oil, ores) much faster than they can be replenished, we destroy.

If we destroy life to save a life, our civilization is doomed to extinction, as plant and animal species are doomed when they disturb the fragile harmony of the whole.

Aboriginal people of the world will be as extinct as tigers will someday be. Tiger tissue may be frozen in the hope that future generations can re-create these animals. A few tigers may be kept alive in zoos. But only a Westerner could think that a tiger could exist apart from his own unique environment and still be tiger. The belief that we can save tigers by freezing some cells is the very belief that is destroying the tigers' habitat: the belief that we are separate. A habitat is more than an *environment,* something to be exploited. In fact, the tiger and the jungle are one; each cannot exist without the other.

The
People

T hey call themselves Sng'oi, the People (also spelled Senoi, though Sng'oi, with its glottal stop, sounds more like they themselves pronounce it). Others have different names for them. Anthropologists and government people call them aborigines, some people call them Sakai, and others call them the Little People. They are elusive and shy. The people of the country among whom they live call them Orang Asli, the Ancient Ones, because they are thought to have lived on the Malay Peninsula from ancient times.

I had heard of the aborigines, of course, when we moved to Malaysia—they were a mystery. Few people actually knew them; they hardly ever came down from the mountains and the deep jungle where they lived. The government estimated there were no more than thirty thousand of them left—and I was told that this was probably a grossly exaggerated number. Government people showed me a map that illustrated where the three aboriginal tribes were. It indicated fairly large areas right through the middle of the country. There were no roads anywhere near.

I first met a few of these aborigines when I visited

anthropologists who were studying their language. This Sng'oi village was large, just off the highway. It was quite different from those I would visit later. This was a show-place. There were perhaps thirty or more people living in the community—at least twice the normal population of an aborigine settlement. The Sng'oi, as is true of many aborig-ines, do not have settled villages; they are seminomadic, moving every few years.

The people in this particular village were used to having visitors. They had lost some of their shyness. We had din-ner, a mixture of imported canned food and rice (not the usual fare, I would learn later). I noticed that very few of the People were eating—the meal had been prepared for the two anthropologists and myself, it seemed.

During and after the meal the anthropologists talked ani-matedly with their informant, a bright, older man with a wonderful twinkle in his eye. The little house in which the anthropologists lived was quite dark and crowded with peo-ple. The scientists' voices sounded loud in the small space. Sometimes I felt husband and wife were competing with each other to make points. I did not listen to what they were saying because it sounded very technical. Although I was not interested in the fine points of linguistics, later I wished I had learned some of the language when I had the chance!

The people of the village were soft-spoken and—the strangest thing—there was usually a little pause before one of the people in the group would say something. I had the odd feeling that they consulted with each other, and per-haps designated one person to speak for all of them.

After dinner the conversation became even more ani-mated; the hut reverberated with talk. I looked around and noticed that altogether only three people spoke: the anthropologists and the informant. The village people seemed to have disappeared, or perhaps they were invisible against the dark walls of the little hut.

One tiny village woman was cleaning up after the meal. She scuttled here and there, collecting plates and the cooking pot, sweeping the mats on the floor. She was so silent and unobtrusive, however, that it was a few minutes before I realized what she was doing. She did not make a big show of her work; she made herself almost invisible. When she came close, I whispered to her. She hunkered down near me, with a cup in one hand and the soot-black pot of rice in the other. I asked if she lived in this house.

She smiled a radiant smile and said, "Oh, I live in the house over there." She motioned with her head over her shoulder, pointing with her lips. "I always clean up. If I did not clean up for them, the house would be eaten by ants and other animals. But don't tell her—she thinks she is keeping house."

When I first arrived, the anthropologists had mentioned how much work it was to live as the natives do because everything was so primitive, but, the wife added, it made her feel close to the women.

I should have lost interest in the People. My first visit had been rather boring and frustrating. It had confirmed my perception of anthropologists as people who argue fine points of Western scientific theory without learning much about the people they are studying. I had learned almost nothing about the aborigines during that visit, and yet I was strangely drawn to them.

A few days later I met a schoolteacher whose mother was an aborigine. He allowed that he did not usually advertise his connection with the aborigines, but he sometimes acted as a sort of liaison. If I were interested, he could tell me some things about them.

We talked about his mother's people, and very hesitantly he told me where there was a real settlement—most aborigines live deep in the jungle, never close to a road. He gave me directions and told me to park the car at a little Chinese store about one hundred miles from where we lived. "Ask at the store," he said, "and they will tell you where to find the path that leads to the settlement."

I asked a friend to accompany me. We found the store easily and asked about the path. It would be about an hour's walk, they said, but simple to find.

After walking perhaps an hour and a half, we knew we were approaching a village when we heard voices, laughter, and people singing. We were tired and hot from our trek through the jungle but felt refreshed when we heard those joyful sounds.

When we arrived, however, the village was totally deserted. Not a soul was to be seen; not a sound could be heard. Six empty huts stood randomly around a clearing. Since the People moved around, these shelters were minimal structures, built high off the ground and accessed by a steep ladder. Sng'oi shelters are used only for sleeping. Life is lived outside, in the open during daylight.

Because we were tired, we decided to wait, thinking the people of the village would return soon. We talked softly—neither of us wanted to break that reverberating silence. An hour passed, then two hours. We waited the rest of the day. Shortly before sunset we saw the face of an old man peeking around a hut. He came forward very shyly, and we looked at each other for a while. I said, in Malay, hoping he would understand, "We came to visit. I have met other Orang Asli and wanted to learn more." I mentioned the teacher who had told us about this village.

He motioned for us to sit down while he sat across from us. He smiled the sweetest smile, and very softly he made it known that since it was dark, it was too late for us to leave anyway, so we might as well stay the night.

He welcomed us in a mixture of Sng'oi—a language has a fascinating rhythm and many glottal stops—a few words of Malay, and signs.

The man was not really old, I discovered—perhaps in his early forties—but very wrinkled. He was a perfect host: self-possessed, calm, dignified. When he stood up he gave a hand sign and suddenly from all around us a dozen or so people came out, including some children.

By this time it was dark. Someone made a little fire. They cooked some rice—which, I learned later, is not their staple, but they had some in this settlement for special occasions. We had brought some cans of sardines (my teacher friend had told us to bring food and that sardines would be especially appreciated). Someone put some vegetables on top of the rice that was cooking.

In the anthropologists' village someone had made a speech to us before dinner, apologizing for the poor fare, for the poverty of the village—a common enough ceremony in that part of the world, and a ritual that usually precedes a meal with important visitors. Here, the old man simply motioned for us to sit around the little fire and eat. They ate rice and vegetables; we, the visitors, ate rice and sardines. I tried to make them understand that we had brought the sardines for them, not for us. It took quite a while for them to understand—and accept—that we did not bring the sardines because we did not trust the food they would prepare for us.

On subsequent visits to this and other villages I did not bring sardines or other gifts of food—or if I did, I did not offer them until after the first meal.

We stayed most of the next day at the little village and had a wonderful time. The second day they all sang again, laughed, and made jokes. I felt honored to be so accepted. But, then, I had hopelessly fallen in love with them. They were the most unusual people I had ever known. They had no neuroses, no fears (except of strangers, perhaps). They had an immense inner dignity, were happy and content, and did not want anything.

At that first settlement, communicating in a mixture of words and gestures that people use when they do not know each other's language yet, we learned about who they were. I should also get to know others of the Sng'oi, they said, and then told us how to walk to another settlement, not too far away.

And when, later, we did go to that other village, someone there suggested yet another. We were passed along, from one village to the next. That first settlement, however, I would return to many times. The people there became special friends.

✠ ✠

I could not, however, spend all my time walking from one village to another. I was working and wanted to spend time with my family. But there were weekends, or days, that I could make free.

On one of my visits I was accompanied by the teacher. We went to a far settlement that neither of us had been to before. It was quite a walk, at least four hours, and included much climbing. The settlement was located high in the mountains.

Until then, there had always been someone who would be sitting by the side of the path as we arrived at a settlement. But when we approached the mountain village, no one was there to welcome us, and even when we got to the little settlement itself, it was remarkably quiet—no singing, joking, laughing. The few people who were around did not hide from us, though, and when we asked them what was going on, they told us that a small baby—only two days old—had died that morning. Everyone in the village was very sad, they said.

My friend the teacher suggested we go to the home of the baby. I did not want to intrude on someone's grief, but he assured me it was all right. When we came to the hut where the little baby had died, there were people standing outside who made room for us.

In this settlement, the houses were built quite high. There was a steep notched bamboo that one climbed to get to an open porch, maybe two feet wide and four feet long. As my head came above the floor of the porch there was a gasp from the four or five people sitting there. Then the teacher climbed up behind me and said, "It is all right; he is one of us." They made room. We sat around the tiny body lying on a little pillow.

Nothing was said.

It was obvious who the parents of the little baby were. They seemed no older than sixteen, perhaps. The mother sat in what was almost a fetal position, all closed in. Tears rolled down her face every now and then. She made no effort to hide them or to wipe them away. The boy, the father, sat next to her. He looked at his dead girl child with an expression of such sadness that it wrenched my heart. Occasionally he would lean over and stroke his wife's hair, or hold her hand.

We were allowed to share their grief. It was a gentle grief—no loud sobbing, or tearing out of hair, but obviously a deeply felt pain that would leave a scar on their memories. I tried to imagine what it would be like to have to return the gift of a first child a few days after her birth.

Finally, perhaps an hour after we had sat down on the porch, a middle-aged man sat up straighter and asked whether someone had a box to bury the little body in. Someone handed up from the bamboo ladder what looked like a shoebox made of split bamboo. A few people left the little porch and others came up, among them an older man and woman, the parents of the young mother.

There was some talk I could not follow. The teacher softly interpreted for me: the baby had to be buried with something that had been close to her during her two days of life. The only thing that had been close was the pillow she was lying on—a square about twelve inches on a side, woven of very fine matting.

"Too bad to bury that new pillow," someone said. The pillow was new; it could be used again.

In the end someone suggested that actually it was not the pillow that had been close to the dead baby, but the little cloth that had covered the pillow. With a feeling almost of relief at this solution, the baby was laid in the box (it had no lid) and someone picked up the cloth to put on top of the grave.

The middle-aged man, obviously a priest or shaman, carried the box through the village. We followed in a ragtag procession behind him until we came to the edge of the village, where some teenaged boys stood around a hole they had dug. The shaman, carrying the box, waited until all of us— maybe a dozen people—had assembled around the little grave. Then he stepped into the hole, the box under one arm, and he talked to the little child:

"You. We are sad to say good-bye to you. You made such a long journey to come to us, nine months in the dark. And then, when you come out, you have to leave so soon. Here"—he reached into the earth to scoop up a little soil— "this is dirt. Dirt is what the world is made of. You have never tasted dirt, but that is what this world is." He gently put some dirt on the lips of the tiny body. "Here, taste it. At least you will have had a little taste of this world, before you go back again. Your mother is sad to see you go so soon. Your father is sad. We are all sad, but we know that you have to go." There was a pause. Then, "We let you go."

The shaman, who had been stooped over the box, straightened up. He looked at the three or four boys who stood at the edge of the grave and addressed them. The tone of his voice changed, becoming strong and loud: "You, boys, listen well to what I am saying. Remember this because when I am gone, you have to carry on. Do you hear me? Are you listening? Pay attention, *you who have to carry on.*"

He put the box in the grave and quickly covered it with a little dirt. The boys shoveled more dirt with their bare hands, until the hole—a small hole for such a small body— was filled. The handkerchief-sized cloth that had been close to the baby was placed on top of the dirt. More dirt was put on the cloth, then stones were put on top of the little mound. We left.

✠ ✠

The People are ancient. They are preindustrial, preagricultural. They are seminomadic and rarely plant crops. Instead they harvest what they need from what grows wild in the jungle around them. When the little clearing they make for a settlement becomes too overgrown, and when the jungle in the vicinity no longer provides what they need, they move.

Their ways have not changed much in a long time. They have few of what we call material goods; they do not need them and they do not want things they would have to carry when they move. Those I knew seemed healthy, although they do not live long, according to our standards. They die from diseases they never knew before, diseases for which they have no natural immunity.

Those I knew kept themselves apart, although the world intruded. The jungle they felt themselves a part of was being clear-cut and planted in rubber trees and other cash crops. Every year the jungle they lived in grew smaller.

Once, when I walked with a young man from one village to another, we talked about their shrinking world. I asked him about the changes he had seen in his twenty-three years. At some point in the discussion, when the difficulties and problems he listed seemed overwhelming, I blurted out, "But what can be done?"

He smiled that achingly sweet smile that I associate with the People—we who are civilized do not know such smiles anymore—and he said, simply, "Oh, we are dying out."

That is what I sensed he said. Literally, what he said was, "We are dead," or, perhaps, "We died." We were speaking a very simple version of Malay, in which there are no clear tenses. Whether a speaker means past, present, or future is for the listener to determine from the context. I sensed that he meant *We are dying out.*

✠ ✠

Today I reflect on the peoples of the world who are extinct. I am saddened to think that humankind entered a new century leaving behind the cultures, the creativity, the wisdom, and the smiles of people we have so thoughtlessly exterminated.

Whether we know it or not, we are their heirs. We must not squander that heritage.

We can't forget; it is we who have to carry on.

The Real World, the Shadow World

Some people—and they are the people we think of as the poorest—live well without doing much of anything. They do not have jobs, they do not work nine to five, they certainly do not work for anyone else. They do not farm; they do not have to take care of animals. They spend their days doing what they do best. Some like making things— they make canoes, or cloth, or pots, or carved objects. Some like hunting or fishing. Some people have a talent for staying in touch with another reality; they are priests, shamans, or healers. Some have a talent for making other people feel good. People who live very close to the earth or the ocean, with very few of what we think of as necessities of life, live well. Sadly, it is no exaggeration to say that as soon as we come and bring them civilization, they plummet into abject poverty and ill health.

The people I knew—aboriginal people in Malaysia, wonderfully healthy and self-sufficient aboriginal people on a few islands of the Pacific and in the mountains of the

Philippines—were different from each other. They spoke different languages, had different customs. But they were alike in that they were happy. They were content.

These people were hard to find because our aggressive and intense civilization had driven them to the most inaccessible parts of the world. They lived off the land or the ocean. They did not have to rely on the outside for any of their needs. They could find all the food they needed to sustain themselves, they could find or make material for shelter and clothing. They carved canoes and made blowpipes, they rolled a powerfully strong rope from the fibers of coconut husks. And beyond what they could find and make in their environment, they did not need anything, nor did they want anything more. They lived life. Life did not live them, as it does us. They enjoyed each other and constantly reinforced the bonds they had with each other by touching: They huddled around a little fire, they slept in a big ball, they often fed little tidbits of food to each other, and they combed each other's hair. In that they were like animals who groom each other.

❈ ❈

The Sng'oi I knew could not read or write. They had no written language. They had a limited knowledge of what went on in the world outside—while they knew the large facts of history as it was played outside of their world, they were not aware of the details.

They obviously did not have an abundance of things. In fact, I learned that they did not have *any* things; they thought the idea of owning anything quite absurd. What few things they used, they made themselves, with some exceptions: they did trade for cloth occasionally, although obviously not very often because each person wore only one little rag. Every settlement probably had at least one pan. They had some knives and *parangs* (machetes), but little else—except hats. Some people liked hats, and had found or traded for the most unusual hats I had ever seen.

The aborigines form a minuscule minority of the population of Malaysia. They are thought to be the original population, the people who had been there before the "native" population of Malays, but there are so few of them left that often they are not counted. More important, they are not Muslim in an Islamic state. It seems the official government intention is to integrate them into the Malay population, even though ethnically, culturally, and linguistically they are not Malay.

I was in Malaysia to study Malay dietary behavior (as one wit said, "To find out why they eat what they do and not what they should"). The first thing I learned was that I must unlearn many of the standard assumptions Western scientists make when they get to know people in other cultures. Malays do not eat three meals a day; they do not eat bread for breakfast or sandwiches for lunch; they do not eat salads. They do eat rice at every meal—and they usually eat two meals a day, not three. These meals are not often sit-down, family occasions. The Malay concept of family is what we would refer to as extended family. In the Malay villages I have visited, other villagers were thought of as family. Children, drifting around in small bands where younger children were helped along by older children, would eat whenever they were hungry, wherever they could find something to eat. Children also often slept wherever they found themselves when they were sleepy.

We discovered that the Malay diet was simple and adequate for the most part, although deficient in certain vitamins. (That was one of the goals of our research; our studies confirmed what was suspected.) These deficiencies were not because there were no foods in their environment rich in these specific vitamins, but the result of beliefs they held about food.

While working with nutritionists and dietitians in the field, I learned that these food- and meal-preparing professionals almost without exception had the notion that once you tell people that they must eat more foods rich in, for instance, vitamin A, they would do so. But strongly held beliefs about food, or anything else for that matter, do not change because someone tells you that you should do this or that. We who are trained in Western universities, where knowledge is imparted as bits of truth, learn soon enough when we get out into the real world that people in general do not view the world as ruled by the kind of logic we learn in school.

Later, when I came to know the Sng'oi, I had to unlearn more. Like Malays, the Sng'oi I knew did not sit down together for a meal (except for very special occasions), but their definition of *family* was quite different from that of the Malays, and something we would not recognize. In a real sense, every human was family to them.

The Sng'oi ate the way nutritionists suggest people suffering from ulcers should eat: they snacked. As they wandered around during the day, they dug up a root here, picked some fruit somewhere else. Often, as I would accompany one or more people on these daily wanderings, each would chew on a root for a while and then store it, usually in a tree, "so that someone else can find it when he is hungry," they would tell me seriously. When I asked whether that someone else might be an animal, they said, "Oh, sure."

I did not see them eat meat as a regular part of their diet. They set traps at times and occasionally someone would be moved to go hunting. When they did come back with meat, all the people who were in the settlement at that time would share whatever was the catch of the day.

Small monkeys were a special treat, I was told. Cooking these monkeys was rather casual; not much preparation was required. They slit open the belly, removed the intestines, left most of the remaining organs in the body, and threw the whole carcass on a little fire. The fire would singe most the hairs off the skin (*because the hairs stick between your teeth,* they said).

I had never been much of a meat eater and I did not share much of the meat they cooked during one of my visits, when a young man had caught two monkeys. After the group was through, though, almost all of the meat was gone, without much left. As do most meat eaters, they ate everything except hair, skin, and bones (although they sucked out the marrow of the bones). Among meat eaters we Westerners are the exception, I imagine, in our wasteful preference for muscle meat only.

A choice part of the monkey, they said, was the hand, and particularly the thick part of the thumb. A monkey's hand looks like a very small human hand, with long, very human-looking fingers. When I was offered that little hand, chopped off just above the wrist, I declined.

The Sng'oi often chewed on leaves. They ate fruit when they found it, as well as insects, grubs, and other things I had never thought of as food. I learned, for example, that flying termites, lightly fried in their own fat, are a true delicacy. On the whole, not a bad diet.

A few settlements had little gardens, for someone who wanted to grow sweet potatoes, for instance, and was interested enough to protect them from other creatures who might want to nibble. Generally, however, they did not grow food. Anthropologists categorize aboriginal groups as hunter-gatherers. During the time I was with them, I saw much gathering and very little hunting.

I did not even try to figure out what their diet would be in terms that Western scientists could understand, counting, for instance, daily caloric intake and percentages of vitamins, protein, carbohydrate. For people living in the mountains, salt was difficult to get. Some settlements had a small container of dirty salt and occasionally someone would go over and take a lick. When people do not cook food on a regular basis, if meals are not prepared for a known number of people, if there is no regularity in what people eat from one day to the next, none of the categories of scientific nutrition is applicable. Yet, obviously, they had survived on this diet for many centuries.

The Sng'oi I knew were physically spare. They were short, maybe five feet tall. I never saw a fat person; they were well muscled, but sleekly so. They were quite vague about how old they were in years—in the tropics there are no seasons to help keep track of such things. I did not see any very old people, however, although many people were quite wrinkled.

I learned to question my own assumptions about many things. I threw out, for instance, the notion that if the machines we think necessary for survival are not available, then we must have to work very hard. The Sng'oi had all the time in the world. They were active all day until midday, but after, when it became hot, they rested. Most of the people I knew lived in the high jungle, in the mountains, where it did not get as hot as it did down below, but was warm enough to enjoy sitting in the shade of a big tree. They did not slave in gardens; they did not work to get ahead; they were not stressed by keeping office hours or schedules. There was nothing they had to do. They enjoyed living; they smiled a great deal, and laughed, and made jokes.

This led me to throw away as well my idea that people who do not have the advantages we have—our many choices of education, infinite forms of entertainment— would have to work so hard that they had no time for fun. They sang almost all the time—little tuneless tunes. Occasionally another person would join in—which was quite a feat because as far as I know they did not sing a known tune. Even two and rarely more than two people singing together always sounded harmonious. Sometimes they made up words as they went along, which almost always led to much giggling and laughter.

What remains most vivid in my memory of the Sng'oi is their contentment, their *joy*. Voices were never raised in anger. They had the uncomplicated innocence of children, although they certainly were not childish or even innocent. There was sadness sometimes, and they freely expressed that, but they most often expressed joy.

✻ ✻

In time I grew to know them better. But it was when I began to overnight in their villages that I learned that they literally lived in another reality. When it became dark, people huddled together for warmth and companionship. In the tropics there is no long period of dusk; it grows dark quickly. The air would become cool and people would move closer together, reaching out, touching a neighbor, perhaps holding hands. Women might run their fingers through the hair of the person sitting next to them.

During the nights I stayed over they would often gather around me and have me ask them questions. Then they would ask me questions, very quietly and softly. Our being together was not like other social situations I had experienced. We talked—but softly. They did not know how to compete for attention. A few words now and then were all that were spoken—a question, or a comment, a simple answer. Long silences. Sometimes someone would have some tobacco and light a "cigarette" (tobacco rolled in a leaf), which was passed around the group. People might ask each other whether they had noticed that particularly bright patch of sunlight on the side of the river, behind a certain tree, or if they had noticed the large yellow bird that sang that morning.

Evening was a time of reflection, of gentle communication, of being together. I never knew their blood relationships, but evening times felt like family.

As it grew later, one by one people would get up, go into one of the houses (often little more than lean-tos, or rickety huts on stilts), and fall asleep. Eventually each of us had found an empty spot on the floor of one of the shelters, and, wrapped in our sarongs, we huddled close to whoever else slept in that house that night. The houses did not belong to anyone—it seemed that each of the four or five little shelters was for all of the people living in that settlement at the moment. We would fall asleep wherever we chose to go—and, I am sure, with whomever we wanted to spend the night.

Yes, people had sex, but even that was gentle, quiet, and discreet. Occasionally someone might turn over and bump into a couple being a little too acrobatic or noisy, and there would be a grunt. Or people might move away from a couple that made too much to-do about their lovemaking. Passionate lovemaking between young people most often took place during the day— outside in a more hidden spot in the jungle, I was told.

In the morning, we might not all wake up at the same time, but those who woke up early would lie quietly, waiting for more people to awaken. And somehow, as if by magic, we would find ourselves sitting in a circle, rubbing our eyes, stretching to get the kinks out. One person would say, "I saw a bird, a beautiful bird." Someone else would say, "Yes, I too saw a bird." "What kind of bird was it?" another would ask. And so we would create a story with images from our dreams.

They did not think that they were sharing dreams as we think of dreams. The Sng'oi believe that the world we live in is a shadow world, and that the real world is behind it. At night, they believe, we visit that real world, and in the morning we share what we saw and learned there. The story that was created around the memories that four or five people brought back from the real world set the tone for the day.

Sometimes one of the group would take the lead in soliciting input from each person in the room: How about you? What do you remember? Other times the story flowed without help. A few times no story emerged at all. It was very obvious that when a more or less coherent story was created around the images we shared, we who had slept in that shelter would *live* that story that day. Usually the stories were simple: a bird had shown the way to a tree that was bearing fruit. Later that day some of us would find that tree, and of course it did have ripe fruit. Or the story was about a bad storm. People would stay close to the shelters all day, and, yes, there was a big storm in late afternoon.

Occasionally the stories were about things that affected all of them, all the people in that settlement, or perhaps even all the Sng'oi. In that case they would make it a point to share with the people who had slept in other shelters as soon as possible. It might take all morning to disseminate the story to everyone. I did not witness any attempts to call a meeting, but it was obvious that when a serious story came out of a morning's dream telling, all the people in the settlement would eventually hear that story.

I learned about all this very early during the time that I spent with the Sng'oi. It was in what I thought of as First Village, the first settlement I visited, that an important story emerged from what I brought back from the real world during one of my nights there. It made a big impression on me because part of the story came from my dream. It was a particularly vivid dream about one of my family's dogs, an all-black mongrel that seemed to have come with the house we rented in one of the suburbs of Kuala Lumpur. We had tried to get rid of the dog—in fact, one of the first days after we moved in, we had run over the poor dog in our driveway—but he would not leave. We tried chasing him away; he kept coming back. So we adopted him and called him Jaga, which is Malay for "guard'" or "protector." I do not remember that Jaga was a particularly good watchdog, but he was around.

In my dream, Jaga, who was a very quiet dog, had barked so loudly that I went outside to see what could be going on.

I could not see the dog anywhere, which left me with a strange feeling of foreboding. I woke up uneasy and shared this dream. One woman said it was a warning dream. All agreed it was a good dream, but they wanted to know more. Since I could not see the dog in my dream, it must have been a spirit warning, they said. The woman who sat across from me (there were, I think, five of us altogether in the shelter that morning) asked what I had done after going outside and being unable to see the dog. I tried to remember more details. It had not been an unpleasant dream, but yet in a strange way . . . yes, I had felt it as a warning. I could not remember what I had done in the dream after going outside and not finding Jaga. It had been dark there.

"Of course, the dog is very black," I said.

"Was it night?" the woman asked.

"Yes." Now I remembered. "It was very early morning."

Everyone nodded knowingly; that meant it was a warning for this day. A man who sat to the left of me asked if it was a continuous barking or a few sharp barks.

Before I could answer, the little girl who sat to the right of me said she too had heard that sound, but she had thought it was a tiger coughing.

We all sat silent. Then I remembered: it *had* been a sharp bark. In fact, it could well have been the cough of a tiger rather than Jaga's rather shy bark. Tigers have many voices—the roar that we often associate with them means one thing, while a sharp coughing sound means something else. Indeed, it could be a warning.

There was silence in our group. I was thinking that perhaps a tiger had been outside in the night, that I had heard its bark and had created a dream around the sound, making the tiger's cough into the bark of our dog Jaga.

As if he had heard my thought, the man to my left spoke up and said, "No tigers have been seen around the village for a while now, but of course it is always possible." Then he turned to me and asked whether I had ever dreamed of a tiger before.

"Yes," I told him. In fact, I dreamed of tigers not infrequently. I was a little embarrassed, but I admitted that I like tigers. They all smiled.

"In that case," the woman said, "the warning is for you, and not for us."

She looked around our little group and asked if anyone else remembered any kind of warning. None of the others reported hearing anything—only the little girl had thought it had been the bark of a tiger.

Other people spoke up: "There are many other animals that make a coughing sound." This was followed by demonstrations of the sound of a pig and other animals. No, the little girl said, quite seriously, she really thought she had heard that tiger sound, but as if it were very far away.

"In that case," said the woman who had taken on the role of interpreter this morning, as she turned to the little girl, "it means that you heard the warning that Bah Woo heard." (Bah Woo was the name they called me at that time.) "You heard the warning that was meant for him." She turned to me then and said, "Maybe the danger is at your house, not here."

All of the people in the circle looked at me with compassion. The man on my left put his hand on my arm and said, "Somebody at home needs you."

I could not call home, so I left soon after. When I arrived home, I learned that one of my children had a medical emergency. I was glad I had listened and hurried.

❧ ❧

There is something very powerful about discussing memories from the real world with a group of people that you have spent the night with, huddled together. Putting it in the context of Western thinking, I have come to think that it is not at all impossible that people sleeping so close together share some of their dream content. I have come to agree with the Sng'oi that when we sleep, we visit the real world, and when we can bring experiences back from there, it may help us live our day in this shadow world.

In fact, even when I was far away from the Sng'oi, I got used to spending a few minutes every morning, before getting on with the business of the day, remembering what I could of my experiences in the dream world. Doing it by myself did not work as well as doing it with a group of people, but often I discovered a message, a theme that colored my day.

Several months later I had a very unusual dream, when I was the advance scout for the nutrition survey. I had felt increasingly stressed by the way the survey was conducted, and my role was becoming almost unacceptably embarrassing to me. I continued my work against my better judgment—I simply did not know how to say no. I felt that some of the scientists who had planned this survey were not concerned with the ethics of the project, nor with the people they used.

My dream occurred toward the end of the survey, when my feelings were anger, frustration, and embarrassment. The dream was a dark one, a nightmare; it woke me from a troubled sleep. Though vague, it scared me—I could not say why. I decided to imagine that I was sharing it with a group of people in a Sng'oi settlement. I could not do much with the dream by myself—I was too shaken with a sort of nameless dread—so I conjured up a sharing with some people I remembered.

In the dream I was traveling somewhere at great speed, at the wheel of a car that was not my own. I could not remember where I was going, although the feeling I was left with suggested I might have been fleeing from something. It was dark in my dream.

This is what my imaginary sharing produced: A young woman whom I imagined sitting next to me began to shiver and said, "I too remember a dark place, and it was cold." Yes indeed, it had been cold in my dream as well.

Then an older woman whom I imagined sitting across from me said she had come back from a place that was dark and cold, and a voice had talked to her—but, she added, not a human voice. A sigh went through the group (I imagined six people around me). Yes, others also had heard a voice that was not human. "A ghost voice," somebody whispered.

They all turned to me and asked me to think back—it was very important since it was a spirit voice: What else could I remember?

Slowly details came back. Yes, it was cold and dark and I had heard a voice, a voice from a radio. I explained *radio* to my imaginary friends: a disembodied voice coming from a machine. The voice belonged to a person far away, not a ghost.

A young man spoke up and said that the voice from that box was probably the voice of government. Did I think the voice had been the voice of government?

Yes, now that you mention it, indeed it had sounded like an official warning . . . about a war?

As soon as that possibility occurred to me, I thought,

That is strange—there is no war. Of course, for the duration of the survey, maybe a month at that time, we had been almost totally cut off from the outside world. We had not heard news; we had not even seen newspapers.

The imaginary—but by now, seemingly quite real—woman sitting across from me said, "Go back to driving the car. There was a warning from the government. What did it say?"

Suddenly I remembered the whole dream. It was indeed a government warning over the radio, one of those droning voices that announced some sort of emergency, with instructions to do this or that. It had upset me so much that I was running away madly from my own fear of what the disembodied voice had announced. I tried to explain to my imaginary friends that I was running because I was afraid. Oh yes, they understood that quite well—a sort of panic. Yes, they could feel that. The whole imaginary group was now in a state of suspense. What did this mean for me?

A very young child piped up that she had seen a big black bird. (Children often see birds in the real world.) When asked what kind of bird it had been, she began to cry. "It was not an alive bird," she said, "it was very big, as big as . . . " She could not think of anything that big.

A young woman who sat next to her and to me took her on her lap and comforted her. "What did the bird do?" she asked the little girl.

"The bird pooped," the little girl said, "and the droppings made a bad noise when they hit the ground."

"A bad noise?" someone asked, with almost a snicker in his voice.

"Yes," the little girl said, "the poop went BLAP," and she clapped her hands together. "But much louder than I can make," she added. "The poop went BLAP, BLAP."

The girl was obviously serious. We were all still.

I decided my fantasy sharing had gone far enough. I now remembered my dream, and I could think about it more rationally. The dream had been unpleasant, dark, and cold, with a warning about something that I could not place. A warning about war triggers memories of my five years in Holland during the German Occupation in World War II—a dark, cold, very unpleasant time in my life. I decided that the dream was my way of dealing with my anger and frustration with the survey. Westerners are good at explaining things away, particularly bad things. I tried to go back to sleep, but I could not.

That day the survey team caught up with me, as they did every few days. We had surveyed, I think, eight Malay villages and were now in the northwestern part of Malaysia. We would overnight at a government guesthouse near Alor Star. There were two more villages to do after the one the team was working in that day. They finished in the afternoon.

Late in the afternoon I sauntered through the streets of Alor Star with some of the Malaysian members of the survey team. It was close to sundown. On one street, fortune-tellers were packing up their paraphernalia, making ready to go home for the day. One of them had a bird that would pick a fortune card from a deck, my friends explained. The fortune-teller had just covered the bird's cage when we walked past.

I turned around, curious about the bird. It seemed a very ordinary macaw. The fortune-teller looked at me, scowled, and said it was too late to get my fortune read.

As I turned away he said, in a rush of words, "You have four sons, and you will see them tomorrow."

I remember saying to my friends, "How could that man know that I have four sons? He certainly got that right, but I am not seeing them tomorrow because we have almost a week's more work with the survey before we can go home."

A few minutes later we arrived back at the guesthouse. There was a message for the Americans on the team from the embassy saying that the international situation was tense and uncertain and all Americans should come back to Kuala Lumpur as soon as possible. The next morning before daybreak, a plane would be waiting for us at Penang airport.

When morning arrived, we went to Penang and were flown to Kuala Lumpur.

I did see my sons.

Fortunately, President Kennedy was able to deal with what later became known as the Cuban Missile Crisis.

✻ ✻

Many months after that, when I felt I knew them better, I told a group of Sng'oi about that dream and how I had imagined a group of them sitting around me, helping me figure out what it might mean. It was evening and we were telling stories. They thought it quite unremarkable that I would have a sharing with imaginary people. While they did not like to think about ever being away from their settlement, they would certainly imagine their people around them if ever they were separated, particularly in the morning, when they share what they had seen in the real world.

When I came to the part about the big dark birds whose droppings went BLAP! with a great noise, there was a wave of gasps in the group. If I thought I was the only one who could understand that image, I was wrong. They all seemed to know about planes dropping bombs. There was a long silence. Nobody seemed to want to break the mood. I felt guilty that I had brought my so-called civilized, warring world into their settlement. I worried about people having bad dreams. I tried to change the subject and made a joke about something else.

We did not go to sleep until quite late that night. I slept touched by at least eight arms.

The next morning nobody seemed to have had bad dreams. The story in our hut was light, about a bird that called other birds to come see a huge flower. I did not pay much attention. The story did not seem important to me.

Later that morning the youngest child who had slept in our hut took my hand and said, "Come, let's go look at the flower." For a minute I did not know what flower she meant, but then I remembered the story of the morning. I smiled. I expected her to take me a little way into the jungle, but she took me quite far from the settlement, all the while chattering about the plants we saw, about animals she knew were hiding from us—no, hiding from me. "They do not know you yet," she said. "When you come back another time, you will see them."

After what seemed like a long but leisurely walk on what might have been a path, we came to a sort of clearing. Other people from the settlement were already there, sitting around the edge of the clearing. In the middle was a huge flower on the ground. There was no visible plant. The flower had an extremely bad smell, which did not seem to bother anyone. Its dark pink petals looked and smelled like very old, very rotten meat.

We sat and watched the flower, then we went back, a few of us at a time.

I asked why they came to watch that flower. They could not understand my question. After all, it was in our house that the story had originated when we talked about dreams. Of course they would look; the dreaming had told them to go see the unusual flower.

Later I learned that *Rafflesia* is indeed rare—few people have seen one. It is a parasitic plant that grows in the jungles of Malaysia and Sumatra, has flowers as much as three feet across, and has no visible stems, roots, or leaves. It is not a fungus but a plant and, as the encyclopedia says, it has fleshy leaves that have a penetrating smell. Yes, indeed!

But this little episode left many questions in my mind. How did they know where to go to see this flower? I did not remember anyone talking about *where* it was.

But then I had not paid much attention when the huge flower first came up in our early-morning dream talk. I had not thought it important.

I decided to leave in the early afternoon of that same day. I could just make it to my car before dark, and then it would only be an hour or so until I was home. We stood around saying good-byes. I felt I should apologize for bringing that story about war and planes and bombs. One of the two older men in that settlement took my elbow and we moved aside a little.

"Do not think that we do not know what goes on in your world," he said. "Do not be afraid to tell us things about your world. We would rather—much rather—hear it from you than from anyone else. We need to know."

I looked at him. He seemed deeply in thought. I waited.

"For a long time we could hide from the world," he

said. "We could be ourselves. Soon we will not be able to hide. Then we cannot be People [Sng'oi] anymore."

My memory of his words is *Once we could be lost. Now there is no place left to be lost.* That is what I remember; I never carried a tape recorder.

He paused again, then said again, "We need to know."

He walked away, not looking back.

Reading
and Writing

When we talk about *education* we mean all that is involved in making us fit to live in civilized society. I remember the time I spent with people we would call primitive. They could not read because they had no use for it. That does not mean they were stupid. Being educated has little to do with being intelligent. In fact, the kind of intelligence people need to survive in the wild is usually destroyed by what we call education.

The Sng'oi do not have a written language. Their language is difficult to learn and is related to the Mong-Khmer language family, linguists say. It is not related to the many forms of Indonesian/Malay spoken by the people among whom they live today.

When I knew them, their villages—no more than settlements, really, of four or five shelters that might last the few years the People stayed in one place—were deep in the mountainous jungle in the center of Malaysia, near no roads (although there were one or two settlements close to a road). We had to walk along trails that were sometimes obvious but at other times required a guide. Certainly there were no telephones, no electricity, and no stores nearby—

none of the amenities of life we take for granted.

I wanted to learn the language, so I carried a little note-book in which I would write down Sng'oi words, in the phonetic alphabet anthropologists use. Soon someone asked me about these mysterious scribbles in my notebook. I explained as well as I could that each scribble stood for a sound. By putting the sounds (technically speaking, phonemes) together, I could learn the words of their language. They thought that hilariously funny. They understood well enough that I wanted to learn their language, but why the scribbles? Could I not remember?

It was not the scribbles but my inability to memorize that was hilarious to them. I tried to explain, until a nice man who had not spoken before said he wanted to learn to write. Yes, others said, they did too.

I agreed to teach them. Tomorrow, they said. I knew that that did not mean the next day, but soon.

That evening I thought about how to teach. Each letter stands for a sound, combinations of letters stand for words... I was not at all sure how to go about teaching basic reading and writing. I went to sleep with the comforting thought that they would probably forget about it anyway.

The next day came and went with nobody saying anything about learning to write. They were particularly busy that day because two young men had decided early in the morning to go hunting. The People hunted infrequently, using blowpipes and poisoned darts; more often they made elaborate traps to catch a wide variety of animals. The hunters came back in the afternoon with two little monkeys, which they gutted and put on a fire. The smell of singed hair was overpowering; there was little wind, and it stayed with us all night.

The next morning they said that now they wanted to

learn to write. The entire village sat around—about a dozen people of all ages, including small children.

I wrote in the dirt: *A* stands for the sound *ah*. I scribbled again: *B* stands for the sound *buh*. We all repeated *ah* and *buh* a few times.

"Now put these two sounds together to make a word," I said.

They all sang out *"Ah-buh."* That did not make a word, however.

"Now the other way," I urged.

They said, in unison, *"Buh-ah."* Now faster: *"B-ah."* Hah! They recognized that word (*bah* means something like "mister"). Their name for me at that time was Bah Woo (*woo* was how they heard my last name).

They were delighted. They could write *ba*. They danced around, sang to each other, made jokes. "More," they said. "We want more." So very soon we learned other letters and put them together to make other words.

After the first hour I realized that they were far ahead of me. After all, they knew the language. I not only did not know their language but also was ignorant about how to teach the rudiments of writing. They corrected me when I said a word with the wrong emphasis or the wrong tone. Their language has a variety of strange and harsh consonants that don't exist in Malay, which on the whole is a very "soft" language. Malay/Indonesian is thought to be the mother language of, for instance, the Polynesian languages that have many vowel sounds and few consonants.

It was astonishing how easily and how well all of them memorized. It seemed that anything they heard and understood once, they knew. The first principle of education, we learn, is repetition. A teacher in our world repeats and repeats and repeats until it is drilled into a student's memory—that is how we think we have to teach. The Sng'oi, after seeing and hearing a letter once, knew it. No need to repeat anything.

Later I learned that this is not unusual. People whose minds have not been cluttered with endless facts have no trouble memorizing. That, by the way, is why oral history is probably as accurate as, if not more accurate than what we call history.

After the second hour I became tired; they wanted to go on all day. The excitement never abated. No need to motivate them! The whole day was one hilarious adventure. They would give each other riddles in writing, then laugh. It was the best party they'd had in a long time, they said—better, even, than eating monkey.

✖ ✖

The next day someone asked, very earnestly, "Now what? What do we do with writing?"

What *could* they do with writing? There was nothing written in their language. No state-appointed committee had approved a written language. There were no newspapers, no books, no advertisements, no street names, no maps to read.

They decided they did not need writing after all.

If I wanted to play with those scribbles because otherwise I could not remember—they looked at each other with amazement and giggled again, thinking about my strange inability to memorize—that was fine for me, but they did not need anything to help them remember; they could remember without writing it down.

Learning letters had been fun but now they knew it was not really very useful.

They were right—in their world, it was not.

Trees in the Jungle

An official of one of the government departments said, sounding frustrated, "Next time you visit those people [aborigines], find out why they are so stubborn!"

He explained that Malaysia at the time had a Land Development Scheme that would increase productivity, income, gross national product, in short be of great benefit to the country. Under the scheme, thousands of hectares of virgin jungle were clear-cut each year to be planted in rubber—Malaysia's wealth at that time came mostly from rubber and tin. The government had repeatedly contacted aborigines living in an area that was to be cut, and offered to pay them to tap the rubber trees after they were mature enough to be harvested. It had been explained to the aborigines that the government would cut down the jungle, plant rubber trees, and care for the trees for two years, keeping the ground around them clear of weeds (using arsenic). Then, when the trees were big enough to be harvested, all the aborigines had to do was tap the trees, collect the rubber, bring it to a collection point, and get rich.

Rubber is the sap of the rubber tree. Shallow diagonal

cuts are made in the bark of the tree, and the sap (latex) runs down the cuts and is collected in a little cup. Each day, the latex, which has hardened a little, is collected. Little processing is needed to make rubber, although certainly we have improved on the natural product by adding chemicals. There is some skill involved in cutting the trees, but not much. Cuts cannot be made too deep (the tree might be killed), and today's cut has to be as close to yesterday's as possible, so that every inch of the bark of a growing tree can be tapped.

It seemed like a risk-free offer to the gentleman from the government, and he could not understand why the aborigines consistently smiled and said no thank you. He wondered if maybe I could convince them that it was all for their own benefit to participate in the scheme.

I said I would try.

When next I visited an aborigine settlement and we were sitting around in the early evening, I told them what the government official had told me about the land development scheme and the role they, the Sng'oi, could play in it. What did they think?

As usual there was a long silence. People looked thoughtful but nobody said anything for a long time. I thought that perhaps they had not understood the question.

I repeated, "The government is cutting the forest to plant rubber trees. They ask whether you want to learn to cut [tap] rubber trees to earn money. You do not have to do anything until two years have passed, when the trees are old enough to be cut. All you need to do is make the cuts in the trees"—some people nodded that they had seen it done and knew how to do it—"collect the rubber, bring it to the government, and they will pay you well."

A longer silence.

Finally one man spoke up. As usual, he obviously spoke for the group. He said they had heard about all of this from those in other settlements where government people had come to explain it to them. There was a slight hesitation in his voice, then he continued, "When you cut the forest, and then you plant one tree, you can grow only that one tree. After that the soil is dead."

They all nodded that yes, this was true.

I was not sure I had understood, but that was all they would say. They smiled but they did not answer any further questions.

Back in town, I asked my own questions. The average life span of a rubber tree is forty years, a rubber planter told me. After the first generation of rubber trees, well, yes, he guessed, they sort of let things go after that. But he thought you could probably plant more rubber trees, maybe with some fertilizer added or something. He was not too clear about the future—he was too involved getting as much rubber out of his trees in the forty years that they would grow. To him forty years was more than enough time to make his fortune, retire, and get away from it all.

I went back to the government department that had asked me to explain the scheme to the aborigines. When I gave the very short and rather simple-sounding answer the Sng'oi had given me, it did not make much of an impression on the officials in the room. Their faces showed clearly that they felt this was another typical aborigine evasion and not really an answer.

In the back of the room an Englishman was on the telephone; he joined us a little later. I repeated that the aborigines I asked had said only that "when you cut the forest and grow one tree, after one generation the soil is dead."

He became excited, took my arm, and said, "Come with me."

We got in his Land Rover and went for a short ride to an agricultural research station just outside Kuala Lumpur. On the way there he explained that they had picked a small section of jungle, one hectare (about two acres), and had roped it off, making a grid by marking trees. Now they were doing a census of all the plants that grew in that small area.

When we arrived he showed me the one-hundred-meter (about three hundred feet) by one-hundred-meter square, with lines marking smaller squares. Then he took me into a little shack where they kept the paperwork. They had finished counting the trees, he said, and now were counting shrubs, bushes, and vines. After that, he said, would come the even more difficult job of counting the smaller stuff on the ground the mosses, lichens, and other minuscule plants.

"And," he concluded with obvious regret in his voice, "we cannot even begin to look at the organisms in the soil."

I do not remember the count, but there were, say, three hundred trees there. Then he said, "The most amazing thing is that with all these trees, there are very few species with more than one individual." The trees in the census plot were all different. There were at most two, rarely three of the same kind.

He sat me down; we were going to have a lecture. He explained that because this jungle looks so lush, so rich in plants, all different, most people think it is the soil that is so fertile that it can support all that variety. "Not so." His voice reverberated inside the little shack. "It's not the soil but the variety itself that makes the richness possible. What one plant takes out of the soil," he explained many times in different ways, "another puts back into the soil. It is not the soil that grows this astonishing variety—it is the air and the moisture. Our warm temperatures without extremes, the constant high humidity—these make this variety possible."

He sat back in his chair, our knees almost touching in the small space. "And as for rubber, only growing one generation . . . of course, they are right, those friends of yours. Absolutely right. After forty years the ground is so depleted you could not even grow grass on it. That is an exaggeration—grass grows on concrete—but you see what I am getting at. After forty years or so, that soil is dead."

I began to understand a little more about a people who had a completely different way of seeing the world. Forty years is a long time. I doubt that the average life span of a Sng'oi was much more than forty years. They based their refusal to tap rubber on something that would not affect them in their lifetime. The aborigines were obviously not interested in getting rich, but they cared deeply about their world. They could not imagine being party to a scheme that would kill the soil.

Forty years is too far into the future for most Westerners to think about. We run businesses looking ahead to the next quarter, and governments are run from year to year. Some countries have plans for the future, but I do not think there has been one country, besides China, that ever has had even a ten-year plan. More commonly a country might have a three- or five-year plan. Westerners would grab the opportunity to earn money for forty years. After that, well, something else will come up. We can save for forty years while we get paid well and after that live on the interest of what we saved. It is hard for us to imagine rejecting such an opportunity.

The Sng'oi, however, did not have much use for money.

They did not need it— they rarely went anywhere where they could spend money, and there was not much that they wanted to buy. No, this was about land. They may not have felt they owned it, but it was their world. They could not be a party to destroying the land. They were part of the jungle. They could no more kill the forest than they could destroy their own skin.

They sometimes made jokes about people who felt they could own land. A child had said to me, "How can you own ground? We belong to [literally 'with'] the ground."

Later, much later, another official working for the Land Development Scheme took me aside and asked what I could tell him about this crazy notion that the aborigines did not own land. They said they owned *trees,* after all!

It seems the government had started to clear the jungle somewhere and had been told that a certain tree belonged to an aborigine man. The official did not think that the person who had told him this was the owner of that tree, but apparently the person felt he should protect the tree because he knew it belonged to someone.

Should they have cut around that tree, the official wanted to know? Should they leave that tree, to be surrounded by the rubber they would plant? They were willing to do that, but someone better tell them quick, so that they would know which trees to leave.

I explained as well as I could what I knew about trees and people belonging with each other. It was not exactly ownership, I said.

The government man got very impatient. "Well, is it or isn't it? If something belongs to you, you own it."

I tried to tell him that it was like his name—it belonged

with him, but he could not sell it.

That did not make much sense to the government agent. He was too busy to listen further. As he walked away, he looked back and said over his shoulder, "Tell your friends that if we cut one of their bloody trees, we shall pay them compensation. But they have to ask for it. We have no time to ask around."

Slaves

Modern man has many names: a first name, a family name, often a middle name, his nationality, and more. The nationality occasionally has the flavor of an ethnic identity, but national boundaries—drawn for political reasons, not for reasons of cultural affinity, language, or ethnicity— usually include a hodgepodge of peoples who happened to have been caught within those imaginary lines when they were drawn on a map to make a country. Hence our need to invent names that are more descriptive of who we are. We call ourselves Native American, African American, Irish-Catholic American, Quaker, Mormon, Amish. Or we use words that describe, perhaps more regionally, where we are from: southerner, Californian.

There are still a few people in the world who are survivors of a time when none of those distinctions existed. They think of themselves as the People, and their name for themselves is whatever the word for *human* is in their language.

In Malaysia, a new constitution recognized three large groups of citizens (three different races, the laws of the land said). These three races were ranked more or less in the order in which they had migrated into what was now a country, earlier arrivals having more rights than later arrivals. The Malays were considered the first, although the aborigines certainly predated them in what was now Malaysia. Malays were called Orang Kebangsaan (People of the Nation); aborigines were politely called Orang Asli, (the Ancient Ones) or, in common usage, Sakai (Slaves).

Most Malaysians had probably forgotten that the word they used for the strange, primitive, very shy people living in the deep jungle of the mountains *(sakai)* means "slave." They rarely thought about those jungle dwellers who wore few clothes and were rarely seen anywhere. In fact, the Sakai, the slaves, were an almost mythical people; few Malaysians had seen them.

After I grew to know the Sng'oi, the People, and when I knew they accepted me, I apologized for having spoken of them as slaves before I knew what they called themselves.

We were sitting around the embers of a little fire in the early evening. There was a flickering oil lamp shedding some light on the porch of one of the little shelters. In this settlement there were four houses; no more than fifteen people lived here. After the sun went down, we sat around, talking now and then, mostly just being together.

I had learned a little of their language, I tried to under-stand some of what they were saying, but I never became really fluent. My apology was a simple phrase. I said I hoped they did not mind that I had called them Sakai. I was not sure whether I had said it right, and for a long time there was no reaction at all.

I imagined that I saw smiles on a few faces, but it was dark. I could not be sure. Long silences were not unusual among the People. Often someone would say something that would be followed by silence until, finally, one person would answer. This one person obviously spoke for the group, but I often wondered how he or she knew what to say for the group.

This time, again, one person answered. He—a rather adventuresome young man, I was told later—spoke slowly, simply, for my benefit perhaps. "No," he said, "we do not mind when others call us Sakai. We look at the people down below—they *have* to get up at a certain time in the morning, they *have* to pay for everything with money, which they have to earn doing things for other people. They are constantly told what they can and cannot do." He paused, and then added, "No, we do not mind when they call us slaves."

✖ ✖

Twenty years after I had that conversation, I read what a few authors had written about other aboriginal peoples in other parts of the world. Laurens van der Post, a South African, describes how even as a child he felt driven to learn what he could about "the Bushman" (the word is always singular in his writing). As an adult he is able to arrange an expedition to the Kalahari Desert, where he finds a small band of Bushman. They are a remnant—they had been hunted and killed by the black man as well as the white man in Africa, and not many survived at that time (a few years after World War II).

Laurens van der Post writes that what sets the Bushman apart from other indigenous peoples is that they could not be "tamed." In Africa, if an aborigine is jailed, he died "for no good reason," as white historians would write.

Perhaps aboriginal people are the only remaining wild

humans (wild in the sense of untamed, rather than crazy). Laurens van der Post suggests that these preagricultural people had not been caught in what he calls "the tyranny of numbers," the idea that there is strength in numbers.

Aboriginal people, no matter their homeland, never settle down in permanent settlements. Instead, they roam the landscape, never organizing themselves into a tribe, and never establishing governments with leaders. They are free, and that, naturally, is why they have been hunted down—often ferociously—by "civilized" people everywhere. We may no longer hunt them down today, but we do feel the need to integrate them into populations that are controlled by a government.

The Malaysian aborigines may have been called slaves, but they are among few peoples left on earth who are free.

✠   ✠

After knowing the People for a year or so, they named me. It was not a name that was formally bestowed on me in a ceremony, but was more a nickname. Someone had probably referred to me as Elephant, and the name stuck (for a while, at least).

I did not like the name Gaja. I thought they saw me as lumbering, awkward, and big. I am not big, not massive as elephants are—but I am taller than most of the Sng'oi. My mind was stuck on an image of circus elephants doing silly tricks. I was a slave to my own clichés.

Only later did it occur to me that they may have meant something entirely different when they called me Elephant. They had never seen a circus; they would not know elephants that did tricks. And I did not know what an elephant meant to them until one evening long after the sun had gone down. Only a few people were still awake in the hut where I would sleep that night. There was a slight rustle outside, the sound of someone tiptoeing very lightly through dry grass.

"Elephant," one of the women whispered.

"They are very curious, and they walk very softly," a young boy added, also in a barely audible whisper.

I do not think I said anything, but the catch in my breath must have given me away.

"Elephants are also very careful," the boy said. "They do not step on anything."

The Mango Tree

The People I knew were quiet; they smiled rather than guffawed. They never argued. I remember all our discussions as slowly paced, thoughtful, and strangely orderly, as though people took turns. I cannot remember ever hearing two people speak at the same time. There was always that little pause when everyone looks in the middle distance, then one person will speak as if he or she were the designated speaker, though nobody had said anything. I thought about this new way of talking for many years; I could not let it go. I could not imagine that they were *telepathic,* but they certainly seemed to know each other's thoughts. Of course, they lived together; they were around each other all the time. They must have known each other intimately. I thought that maybe this explained it. But it remained a baffling and confusing fact.

Gradually I came to realize that their world, their reality, was what we would call a spiritual reality; it was not the tangible reality we are more familiar with. It was a reality where things were *known* outside of thinking.

In the two years that I knew some of the People, I visited several settlements, usually—but not always—with someone to accompany me. There were no addresses or maps—after all, they moved about. Usually, someone had talked with someone else, who had talked with someone else, who had seen a particular group of people near a certain waterfall. I could not drive anywhere near where they lived, so we would drive to what we thought might be near enough, park the car—often at a little country store—and walk.

We were always met by someone about half an hour from the village. He, or she, seemed to be waiting for us. As we came along, the person would silently get up and walk in front of us the rest of the way. Not much was said, if anything. The People did not have telephones; there was no way to let them know we were coming on a certain day, in midafternoon. My visits were often unplanned, depending on whether I could get away from home or work. I would decide in the morning, or a friend would show up and say, "Let's go."

How, then, did they know to expect us? But obviously, I thought, they did know. I was grateful. In fact, after the first few times, I expected to be met.

Once I asked the person who was waiting by the side of the path, "Who told you to come out here to meet us?"

Nobody told him, he said.

"Then how did you know to meet us?"

No answer, but a beautiful smile.

I could not understand, and I could not let it be. So another time I asked the person who was waiting, an old man, "Why are you here?"

He looked up with surprise. "To show the way," he said

with a shrug.

We had followed an obvious path for more than an hour. I asked if he thought we would not have found his village without his help.

"Perhaps," he said.

In time there were a few people who became special friends. To one of them I confessed that I was stumped. I could not figure out how they knew things.

He laughed—he could not figure out how we knew things either, he said. The conversation stopped there. A little later he volunteered, "Maybe we do not understand each other because we do not know to ask the right questions."

Yes, that was what I felt many times when I heard those simple answers that did not answer anything at all. Maybe I had not asked the right question. So I said, "One of the things that is hard for me to understand is why there is always someone on the path before I come to a village. How do they know to meet me?"

"They do not come to meet you," he said.

"Then why are they sitting by the side of the path as we come by?"

"They are just sitting there."

"Do you mean, someone is sitting alongside the path for some other reason?"

He did not answer that. Was it my conceit to think they were waiting for me?

I was beginning to feel like one of those stupid dogs that bite and then cannot let go. I turned to my friend and asked him whether he sometimes just goes out and sits by the side of the path.

Yes, he said, he would do that sometimes.

"And then? After a while you just go back and go about your business?"

Yes, maybe. But, he added, usually it would become clear why he was there.

Those were not his words, but that is my interpretation of what we talked about that afternoon. Someone would have an inspiration, let's say, to follow one of the many paths in the jungle. He would have a *feeling*—though that is not the right word, either—to wander. And whatever he or she would find—a particularly wonderful fruit, or a visitor to the village, or an animal, that became the reason for coming that way. Was that how it worked—you followed your intuition and whatever happened was the reason for having the intuition? It was my clumsy Western way of expressing what was not a Western kind of behavior.

The People did not hang around a settlement very much. During the day they wandered here and there, sometimes in small groups of two or three, often alone. I had assumed they were looking for food, because often I would see them munching on something—and in my thinking one always has to *do* something. When I accompanied people, I thought of their wandering as looking for food, but maybe that was just my interpretation, how I perceived what I saw. Maybe they were not doing anything at all, maybe they were just drifting. Food was where they found it. Most of their food gathering was as casual as that, it seemed to me. There were no definite plans; they just floated this way and that.

In fact, when I thought about it, they rarely seemed to *look* for food. They would wander around and look under a leaf, follow a path a little way, every now and then dig and find a root, or reach up and pick a fruit. It all seemed very casual, unplanned. They were happy; it was fun! They would laugh at a small animal tripping over its feet as it scuttled away. They would stop and admire a flower, or a shaft of sunlight through the canopy of the trees far above. Often they would hum a little tune, while they seemed almost to dance from this tree to that bush, do a little step, then move on to another tree. When they were with two or three others, they would rarely talk, but would often hold hands, or reach out to touch a person walking beside them.

Maybe it was just happenstance that when we approached a village there would be someone sitting by the side of the path. Always? By chance? I still do not know.

In my reality it makes no sense. I cannot explain.

In their reality it is what happens.

One thing I did finally understand and accept: they were not waiting for *me*. They were just sitting there as I happened along. Only then did it become clear to the people who were sitting by the path that *to escort a visitor* was why they were waiting. As we came by, they joined us; they showed the way.

When I understood this much about the People, I realized how truly different their reality was. My reality is made in my head; I create roles for myself, I create a structure that requires certain activities and prohibits others. I live in time; I have an agenda.

Their existence had no reality until they lived it.

They did not plan their lives, they did not say to themselves or to each other, *Today we do this or that*. They did not say, *Today we are going to have a visitor* (not an unusual occurrence, by the way—I was astonished to learn how much they traveled, visiting other groups or merely traveling for the sake of traveling).

Each day a blank page, to be written as one lives it.

✠ ✠

I tried to imagine what it would be like to listen to my intuition, inspiration, whatever one calls that inner voice. In my world that is almost impossible to do. We live by schedules, appointments. We eat when the clock says it is time to eat. We go to sleep after the news, which comes on at 10 P.M., or elsewhere at 11 P.M. In my world we cannot live another way. From earliest childhood we are told to plan, to think about the future. We impress upon children how important it is to know what they want. And from the first day of life we are also told that some things are real. Everything else is imagination.

What would it be like to live in a world where I did not need to want anything, where I could let myself drift, a world where food was found, not bought, prepared, preserved, planned? What if I lived in a world where, if an interesting stranger came along I could spend my time with him, because being with a visitor was what I had to do in the moment? What if I too could live in the now?

As a scientist, I decided I had to try. I would have to experience how that felt. I told myself that for one day I would set aside any agenda I might have and would just *be,* as the People seemed just to *be.*

Immediately I discovered that it was extremely difficult to change my usual behavior. It was very stressful not to have an agenda, not to wake up with a clear idea of what I was going to *do* that day. I felt lost, adrift, without the security of a schedule, goals, and objectives.

The first day I tried this experiment, my mind raced all day. I could not stop thinking: *What if—did I forget something—should I do something else—was it time for a meal yet—did I feel tired—maybe I should—what did I feel— what is going on?*

In fact, my mind was so busy that at the end of the day I was exhausted, and I realized that if I did have an inner voice I could not possibly have heard it over the roaring noise of my mind. Gradually, I learned.

There were days when I floated.

The strange thing was that as soon as I could do that, I no longer heard my mind.

To my surprise I started seeing things in my environment that I had not noticed before. I observed insects; I saw a sunbeam sliding around a tree, brilliantly illuminating a little puddle of muddy water. I smelled things I could not name. I heard tiny rustlings as well as birdsong, a breaking twig.

I saw a mango tree not far away with hundreds of ripe fruits that had fallen on the ground, there to be harvested. I had an immediate old-style thought: *must gather as much as I can, because* . . . But I stopped that thought. That was not how one played this game. I reminded myself to live in the moment.

I sucked a very ripe mango and stopped when I knew I was eating more than I needed (I had not yet learned to listen to my stomach).

Sitting down under another tree, I saw ants crawling everywhere. Birds came when I sat still. A snake came to look at the birds. I smelled another animal—I was not sure what. I heard noises that I could not interpret. A new world unfolded for me and in me: I felt I was part of the scene, not just an observer. I belonged as much as the rotting mangoes, or the birds.

When I tried to inventory all I saw, I lost that new awareness. And when I tried to name something I saw or felt or heard, I lost it too. All I could do was experience.

I must have fallen asleep. I dreamed a formless sort of dream, no pictures, no story, just warm feelings. When I woke, I woke easily, immediately. I saw that what I had smelled earlier was a little monkey who was sucking on a mango. I looked up and saw a larger monkey keeping an eye on me and on the little one. We looked at each other, acknowledging each other: yes, you are in that tree—I am sitting here. I see you, you see me.

The writing of the last few paragraphs took minutes; my learning took many months. But like learning to ride a bicycle, once one knows how to let go and *be*—observing from within, as I thought of it, and listening without judging, categorizing, or analyzing—once one knows, it is not difficult to get back there.

✻ ✻

A few years later I was in San Francisco, riding a bus through the Fillmore District at about 10 A.M., a quiet time. The bus was not full. I chose to sit in the back.

At one of the stops a man, perhaps in his middle thirties, got on. He seemed happy. He talked with people, made funny remarks about a hat as he slowly made his way to the back of the bus. His speech was only a little slurred; he was slightly drunk, I thought, but happy drunk. He had a knife stuck in the back of his pants. He made no attempt to hide it, nor did he draw attention to it.

A woman standing in the front of the bus shrieked when she saw the knife. Her screams were almost immediately taken up by others. In seconds panic was sweeping through the passengers: people surged away from the man.

The bus driver, with much screeching of brakes, stopped the bus at an angle to the curb and as soon as he opened the door people pushed and shoved their way out—except the man with the knife and I.

A police officer came rushing to the scene, got in the bus, grabbed the man with the knife, made a big show of disarming him, handcuffed him, then maneuvered him off the bus. He came back, looked at me, and said, "How come you didn't leave the bus, mister? Didn't you see he had a knife?"

Yes, I had seen the knife. A knife can be dangerous, but I *knew* that this man did not think of the knife in this way—there was not a bad thought in his mind. I did not read his mind; I read his posture, his behavior.

"You're crazy, mister," the police officer snarled at me as he left the bus and the passengers came aboard again. The bus driver came on last and looked around to see that all his charges were safe. He looked at me and shrugged his shoulders.

✠ ✠

The People were not ignorant of the world. They knew that we had many things that they did not. They were very selective in choosing what they could use from our world. They did not want transistor radios—they made that clear. Transistor radios were the vanguard of the twentieth century in the most remote areas of the world. The People could, however, use a pot to cook in, although if they had one, they did not want another. They had no use for nails—their little houses were made of bamboo lashed together with rattan. They had knives and parangs. They did not particularly want nylon shirts, although a man who went "down below" (to the lowlands) would usually "find" a shirt to wear. They laughed at shoes; they said they wore out too quickly.

The People thought it *very* strange that others felt they could own land. The People did not own land, but they had trees.

I tried to understand the concept. Language gets in the way. I concluded that what they meant is that a tree and a person might belong together, as my legs belong with me. I cannot sell my legs. Nor can I sell my name. Neither legs nor name can be thought of as a possession. Similarly, someone of the People could not give away his tree or sell it. Trees are not property.

The People had no concept of property. Someone who belonged with a tree could use the fruits of the tree, perhaps the wood itself, but could not dispose of the tree, just as the tree could not dispose of the person. I am not certain how one acquires a relationship with a tree. The only answers I could get to my questions were that everyone knew that certain trees and certain people belonged with each other. Sometimes, I was told, a child who has had a close relationship with an adult who dies young might be given a tree as something like an inheritance.

Once I was in a settlement when a young man came back from a long time of traveling (the Sng'oi version of a vision quest, perhaps, or, more practically, a way to find a wife). The young man did not say much about his travels, but he did mention that he now had a tree. Everyone seemed pleased and praised him.

He told us what kind of tree it was, how old it was, where it was, what it looked like. It was obvious that from now on everyone in this settlement would know that that tree belonged with that young man. And from what I knew of the People, that kind of news would travel very quickly to other settlements.

Belonging with a tree, by the way, also meant that you belonged with the offspring of that tree. Some trees spread their offspring in a neat circle around them, but other trees have offspring that are scattered over a wide area. How could someone know that this tree here is the offspring of another tree that is, say, several hundred feet away? Again, nobody doubted—*Oh yes, we know.*

I wondered whether the mango tree whose fruit I had eaten belonged with someone. I decided to ask one of my special friends. This friend was not from the settlement near the mango tree, and questions that were not about something specific were very difficult to ask, I knew. I could not say, "Suppose I ate from a mango tree that belonged with you?" A "suppose" sentence cannot be expressed very well in simple Malay (and my Sng'oi was never very good).

All I could think to ask him was "Are there trees that belong with you?"

Yes, there were trees that belonged with him . . . here and there. He was vague about the location of his trees, probably because everyone knows, and he assumed I did too.

"Is there a mango tree that belongs with you?"

Yes, he smiled—a very nice tree.

"Can I eat some mangoes from that tree?" I looked away

when I said this, not wanting to embarrass him, or myself.

"Yes, of course," he said. Then he added, "Do you know the tree belongs with me when you eat the mango?"

We were talking in the country language; it was impossible to know whether he said "Did you know" or "Do you know." I am fairly certain however that he meant *did you.*

"No," I said, "I did not know. In fact, I did not know at that time that some trees belong with Sng'oi."

There was another one of those long silences. We were alone, walking in the late afternoon no more than an hour before sunset, when the world is shivering its feathers, getting ready to settle in for night and a new crew.

Finally he said, "We eat mangoes that are lying on the ground. If we do not eat the fruit, it would go to waste. Then," and I swear he said this with a twinkle in his eyes, "little monkey come and suck the very ripe fruit, and an adult monkey watch baby [monkey]."

Yes, probably little monkeys frequently find mango trees with ripe fruit lying on the ground. He did not mean anything with that remark. Was it just a general comment?

I could not drop the subject there.

"Maybe I pick a whole bag of mangoes to take home with me."

"Why you do that?" he asked, with genuine surprise in his voice.

"To share with my children," I said.

Another pause.

"You bring children to tree; they know where find; another time they hungry for mangoes they know where find."

I never knew whether we were talking about an imaginary tree or about the tree that I remember so well, where I had observed a little monkey sucking on ripe mangoes while an adult monkey watched. But I was beginning to get a feeling for his world, a reality that was not exact and measured as our world is.

In his world it was not strange that he sat by the side of a path for no apparent reason, but knew, when a visitor came, why it was that he sat there: to show the way.

Shaman

One of the settlements I called Three—the third settlement I had visited. Generally Sng'oi settlements do not have names; after all, they are temporary. I had been there several times. It was the easiest to reach, only about an hour's walk from where I could park the car. I was beginning to know the people there well, I thought.

Usually there were about twelve people there, though this varied—every time I had gone some people were missing, while others had come whom I had never seen. The Sng'oi were a very mobile people. Personal questions, however, such as "Do you live here?" or "Where do you come from?" were ignored, never answered.

Once, when on my way home from the east coast, where I was doing some research at the time, I came by the little store where I parked to go to Three. Spontaneously, I decided to make a brief visit. I was on my way to Port Dixon, on the west coast. Port Dixon was trying to become a seaside resort, a place to vacation, with cabins to rent and other facilities. There were miles of fine sand beaches, but the ocean (actually the Strait of Malacca, between Malaysia and Sumatra) was so shallow you could not swim there.

There was not much to do other than look at the ocean.

As I made ready to leave Three there were perhaps six or seven adults standing around. On the spur of the moment I asked whether someone would like to go to Port Dixon with me—as you ask a friend to come along. I explained that my family would be there, and other friendly people. We would be gone a day, at the most two, and of course I would return to the settlement whomever chose to go with me.

There was that moment of silence when I imagined they consulted with each other (at that time I thought of it as mind talk). Yes, one man said, he would go with me.

He did not need much time to get ready for the trip other than to get a shirt, but as we were about to leave, a woman came running after us with a pair of slippers. "Here," she said, "you will need these."

Port Dixon was not much of a town and nobody would pay particular attention to a barefoot man. Malays often go barefoot, and he was fairly tall for an aborigine—he could pass for a Malay.

My companion's name was Ahmeed. Much later I learned that this was not his real name, but his public name—what people called him. He did not say much as we walked the path that led to the little store where my car was parked. Nor did he say much as we drove to Port Dixon, perhaps two or three hours from where my car had been parked.

I knew him from earlier visits: he was in his middle years, which meant probably middle or late thirties, and was a man of few words, though with a nice twinkle in his eyes. He laughed easily. As I looked at him, sitting next to me, I realized I knew hardly anything about him.

✠ ✠

We arrived in Port Dixon late in the afternoon. I introduced Ahmeed to the people who came to meet us and he was welcomed warmly. My family and I had dinner outside that evening, looking at the sunset over the ocean. I sat next to Ahmeed, who was very quiet. I thought I could understand why: he was not used to being with so many strange people. It did not occur to me at the time that he might be awed by the ocean.

The sunset was spectacular, the ocean flat; there was almost no wind. That meant lots of mosquitoes.

The next day I woke very early. The beach faces west and south: beautiful sunsets, but no sunrises. It was fairly cool, although there was not much of a breeze. The ocean was flat; there were no waves to speak of. Sumatra must be across the water, I knew, not too far on a map, but the ocean disappeared in a haze of mist and merged into the sky without a visible horizon to mark distance. There was nothing to tell that there was land anywhere other than the land we stood upon.

I saw Ahmeed standing very quietly among the casuarina trees that fringed the beach. I started in his direction, but turned back when I saw how intensely he was concentrating, his face toward the ocean. I was not sure he had his eyes open. It seemed he did not want company.

Later that afternoon, as we drove back I asked Ahmeed if he would mind staying a night at my house, which was about halfway to Three. He mumbled something, which I took for consent. We were living in a suburb of Kuala Lumpur, the capital, in a very large, very Western house, with five bedrooms, four bathrooms, I think, and air conditioners in every bedroom. I showed Ahmeed to the guest room downstairs. He declined to sleep in the bed and said he preferred to sleep on a mat on the floor. I feared the concrete floor would be unusually hard, but he insisted. I demonstrated how to use the air conditioner, but turned it off before leaving him for the night. It would be too cold, he said.

When we were back in Three the next morning, I heard him say to someone, "Bah Woo lives in a big house, with air piped in from the mountains."

In the afternoon, some people gathered around. We talked about the visit to Port Dixon and answered some questions. It got late; I decided to stay in Three that night. I was aware that there were lively discussions among little groups of people, well into the dark of the evening, but I did not intrude.

The next morning, as I was getting ready to leave, a very strange thing happened: Two or three of the oldest people in the settlement came to me. They wanted to talk to me, they said. They seemed almost an official delegation. Haltingly, they explained that Ahmeed on his visit to the Great Water, as they called it, had seen some important things. There would be a sort of ceremony that evening, where he would tell what he had seen. They were not sure what I might think of that, but if I wanted to stay, that would be all right; after all, it was I who had introduced him to the Great Water.

Forgetting other commitments I had at home, I accepted. I am not sure what I expected, but I felt this would be a unique opportunity to learn more about them. In my contact with the Sng'oi, they had been remarkably down-to-earth; there was little talk of ceremony or ritual. They did not say much about their spiritual life, although from the morning sharing sessions I knew that their belief in the dream world, a world they called the Real World, was central to their lives. Yes, I certainly would like to stay another night and be there when Ahmeed reported to them about what he had seen.

As was everything in their lives, the ceremony was the essence of simplicity. They chose the largest house, a structure like all others, raised about six feet off the ground and made of bamboo poles in the four corners, a split bamboo floor (you could see the ground between the cracks), a roof and walls of dried palm leaves, and a tiny door (you almost had to crawl to get inside).

The ladder leading up to the little house—perhaps eight by ten feet—was a notched tree placed at a very steep angle. The Sng'oi, young and old, walked up that tree as easily as they walked on the ground. I had to climb it on all fours, very carefully.

In the middle of the floor a shallow bowl had been placed, with a few pieces of burning charcoal and a few chunks of *damar,* a resin with a strong, pungent smell when burned (similar to *copal,* I have been told, used in Central and South America). A few small children were held by adults in the corners of the little house. I also sat in a corner. Eight adults stood in a circle around the brazier. Ahmeed sat in the middle, next to the smoking brazier, occasionally taking a deep breath of the strong damar smoke that wafted to every corner of the hut. (There were square holes on the sides of the house but they were closed at night; there was no hole in the roof, only the door opening, at floor level, to allow smoke to escape or fresh air to get in.)

The adults began to move counterclockwise around Ahmeed and the brazier, making the house shudder and

sway a little. I had never seen this kind of dancing before—
they were hopping, though not together, very softly on
their toes. They shuffled around for a few minutes before
one man began what I later learned is called keening in
English: a monotonous, very high trilling single tone. Soon
others joined in, more or less together. The effect was of
unmelodious yodeling heard from a long distance, eerie
rather than impressive. I felt chills running up my back and
could not keep my eyes off them. The shuffling dance
accompanied by the strange sounds that never quite came
together was unlike anything I had ever seen or heard and
was fascinating to watch.

Suddenly Ahmeed spoke in an unusually loud and deeply
sonorous voice. At first he remained seated, swaying, his eyes
closed. His voice was different, not his normal speaking voice;
it came from deep in his chest. He spoke with great authority.

He began: He had gone with me to the Great Ocean.
It took a long time to get there; even in a car, it was far
away. There was a slight pause, as if he was thinking how
to continue. By that time I could understand some of
what he was saying; he used many Malay words, which
might have been because their language has no words for
the Great Ocean, as he called it, and many of the other
things he described.

The dancers sat down but continued keening very softly
(it is very difficult to keen softly, I learned later), swaying
their bodies in perfect harmony this time. Ahmeed continued speaking with great authority:

When we had arrived in Port Dixon [he said "the coast"]
and he got out of the car, he heard *shshsh, shshsh,* the sound
of rain when it is still a little distance away, very softly, *shshsh,
shshsh, shshsh.* (He heard the sound of waves on the beach,

INNER TRADITIONS • BEAR & CO. • HEALING ARTS PRESS • DESTINY BOOKS • Park Street Press • BINDU BOOKS • BEAR CUB BOOKS

Please send us this card to receive our latest catalog.

☐ Check here if you would like to receive our catalog via e-mail.

E-mail address _____

Name _____ Company _____

Address _____ Phone _____

City _____ State ____ Zip ____ Country ____

Order at 1-800-246-8648 • Fax (802) 767-3726

E-mail: orders@InnerTraditions.com • Web site: www.InnerTraditions.com

Inner Traditions • Bear & Company
P.O. Box 388
Rochester, VT 05767-0388
U.S.A.

but I knew he had never before seen a beach or an ocean.)

He looked up and said, "There was not a cloud in sight. The sky was clear. Where could that sound come from, *shshsh, shshsh, shshsh*?" He made walking motions to suggest walking a few steps from the car. "And then I saw the Great Ocean: *AAHHhhh*."

Briefly there was total silence, then the people continued their swaying and soft keening.

Ahmeed went on: "There was great fear in this heart." (There is no possessive pronoun in Malay; one cannot say *my* heart.) "So much water . . . Listen! In front of you there is water as far as you can see." And he repeated: "As far as you can see."

The people were silent now, awed and afraid. I could feel their wonder, but also their fear. The Sng'oi live in deep jungle in the mountains. The only water they know is rainwater and the water of jungle streams. Water is feared; rainstorms destroy, mountain streams are unpredictable.

Ahmeed went on: "As far as you can see there is water, and if you stand as far as you can see, there is still more water as far as you can see from there." The people were listening, spellbound. Nobody moved; nobody made a sound. It was as if they were holding their breath.

A few times Ahmeed repeated, "As far as you can see is water, and you stand there—*again* as far as you can see is more water, and *again* you stand where you cannot see any farther—*again* there is water as far as you can see." Then he said, "The water is *everywhere*," ending on a sort of sigh.

Some people were hunched over, cringing from this concept of endless water. Ahmeed said again, "Much fear in this heart," and put his hand over his heart. "Much fear, because all this water eats the land"—just as the water of little jungle streams "eats" the land of its banks when rains swell streams to raging rivers.

There was a long silence. Nobody said anything. More people were hunched over, some holding their hands to cover their heads. A woman, sitting in a corner, holding a small child, crooned softly, "Don't cry, don't cry . . ."

Now Ahmeed stood up straight, looking down at the people of the settlement who were bent over, fearful, silent. He stood for a few minutes, then, in a strong voice, he said: "That night, when I go to the Real World, I meet the Lord of the Great Ocean. *Datok Laut Besar*" (he used Malay words). The Lord of the Great Ocean told him not to be afraid, that the Great Ocean would not eat the land; the land was floating on the ocean.

A sigh of relief went through the people. They looked up, looked at each other. Yes, that was it, the land was floating on the ocean, yes, that could be . . .

Then Ahmeed said a strange thing: "All that water is heavy." He bent over to indicate great weight; you could see his shoulders stoop with the heaviness of all that water. "Heavy, all around the world, very heavy."

He went on, "The whole world is covered with the Great Ocean." He cupped his hands about eighteen inches apart, as if to mark a globe. "All of it covered with Ocean, and the land floats on the water." His body movement suggested that the land was lighter than the ocean; that is why it would float on the water.

"The land is so big, there is so much land floating on this Ocean that it does not move, or maybe only a little, and we do not feel it moving."

There was a long silence, as if to let the people get used

to the ideas Ahmeed had presented so far. He remained
standing; he would continue.

The damar smoke was thick in the little house. A few
people were discreetly coughing behind a hand. My eyes
were beginning to tear. The scent of damar is not unpleasant, but thick smoke in such a small space was getting to be
uncomfortable. I thought that the smoke would be rising,
so I bent down to the floor to get some breaths of purer air
from between the cracks in the floor.

Ahmeed went on, almost conversationally. His eyes were
still closed, he swayed a little, and as he was talking he
seemed to be listening.

"All this water," he said, "and underneath the surface"—
underneath that which can be seen—"is a whole world, in
some ways like this world." He used his hands to accompany his words. "There are mountains under what-can-be-
seen, very tall mountains, some of them." He motioned
high, high up with one hand.

"And there are valleys deeper than any valleys we have here.
All through that Great Ocean there are streams, huge rivers"—
currents—"that flow all around the world, around and
around." His hands went around an imaginary globe again.

"These streams are so immense"—the word he used
means something like "bigger than big"—"that they sweep
all the fish around too. And there are many other animals
as well, not just fish. There are animals so huge . . . bigger
than elephants."

The people made a soft *waahhhhh* sound.

"Animals that are flat"—he clapped his hands once—
"and animals that are like snakes, but bigger, much bigger.
But do not be afraid—the Big Ocean cannot eat the land.

The land floats, and the animals in the Big Ocean can live only there; they cannot come on land." He repeated in a singsong, "Do not be afraid. The Lord of the Great Ocean has told me, do not be afraid because the land floats on the water, and the animals in the ocean cannot come on land."

Many times he repeated that the land floats on the ocean, do not be afraid.

I could not imagine how he might have learned these facts about the ocean and the animals that lived in it in the short time we had been there. Could someone have told him? I did not think so—there had been few people there, and every time I looked for him, he was standing alone under the ironwood trees, watching the ocean. He obviously had not read the information in a book—he could not read. Then where did he get such detailed information about something that he could not have seen with his eyes?

Ahmeed continued, talking again about how large the ocean was, how vast, how heavy, how it went around the globe. He was using the word *dunia*, "world"; he obviously meant *globe*, cupping his hands. He repeated his description of the mountains and the valleys of this world underneath the surface of the ocean that was like our world, but on a larger scale. He repeated his description of the huge rivers that flowed through the ocean, carrying animals with it, and how, when two of these rivers met, there was enormous turmoil, all of it below what can be seen.

While I was trying to grasp how or where Ahmeed had learned so much about the sea in such a short time, I fell into a trance.

It was not the first time that had happened Apparently I hypnotize easily, and I imagine the damar smoke, the close air, the swaying people, the voice of Ahmeed . . . all of these together put me in a trance.

I do not know how the evening ended.

Perhaps an hour later—I am not sure of the time; I never wear a watch—I woke up. The house was quiet and almost empty. Ahmeed held me sitting up, and a woman was sitting in front of me wiping my face with a rag with the smell of damar, mumbling as to a baby.

I was embarrassed. I apologized to Ahmeed, telling him I did not mean to fall asleep, that I had no recollection of what had happened after I had fallen asleep, and that I hoped he would forgive me.

It did not feel as if I had fallen asleep, but here I was, held upright by Ahmeed while a woman wiped my face.

He smiled and said, "Oh no, you did not sleep. You went into a trance: you talked to us." He would not tell me at first what I had said, only smiled.

"Later," he said, "later you will know."

Weeks later Ahmeed told me, when I asked, that I had stood up after he had finished talking, and said something in a language nobody had ever heard before (not English, he thought), and with my hands had made a globe. He had understood me to say that I had traveled around the world. When he had told this to the people there, I had nodded, as if to say yes. Then I had said more things, and pointed up, away from that imaginary globe. He had not quite known what I had meant to say, but he thought I had told them that there are other worlds far away from the earth.

Afterward, the people had gone to the other houses and he and the woman had gently brought me out of my trance.

I felt embarrassed. I certainly never intended to do anything like this. For all I knew I had spoiled their ceremony.
But Ahmeed smiled, and said it was all right.

Shortly after, we all fell asleep. The charcoal had long
since burned down and the damar was burnt up—even the
smell seemed to have gone. I felt cold; I lay down close to
some people who had come back into the house to sleep.
The next morning, when we sat and shared what we had
learned in the real world, everyone had seen or touched or
felt something about the Great Ocean. Ahmeed himself did
not say anything, even when people jokingly said, "You, did
you not go back to that Great Ocean you told us about?"

No, he smiled, he had had learned other things in the
real world, but he would not tell.

I could not remember a single dream, but what Ahmeed
had told us about the ocean kept going through my mind:
How could he possibly have known about mountains deep in
the ocean, the currents, the whales, the flat animals (manta
rays came to mind)? How did he get that information?

✠ ✠

I could not postpone returning to my world any longer, so I
made ready to leave early in the morning. While I said good-
bye, again I saw some of the adults consulting in a little
group off to the side. Again a delegation came to talk to me.
They were not comfortable, I could see. They shuffled,
looked from one to the other.

Finally Ahmeed stepped up to me, very close, looked me
in the eyes, and said, "We talk."

He explained, and the others nodded as he talked, that I
had fallen into a trance last night although I did not make
any effort to do so: not willed or not wanted, he said. If I

were Sng'oi, that would tell the others that I was meant to be
. . . Here he paused, as if he could not find the right word.

Then he said that he, Ahmeed, was a bomoh (the word
he used is a Malay word that means "healer"; it might even
be used for shaman). I must have looked surprised. After
the evening's ceremony it was clear that he was a shaman
perhaps, but not a bomoh. I knew what a bomoh did, and
it was obviously not what Ahmeed did. He was not a
healer—or was he? I was confused.

He smiled. "You did not know that," he said, but that
was why he had come with me to Port Dixon. "It is my
work to bring new knowledge to the People."

The subject had not come up before, and I did not know
that the Sng'oi had . . . what? Priests? Shamans?

In fact, Ahmeed avoided using a name for what he was.
When I pressed him, he would say bomoh, probably
because he knew—I had told him—that I was making a
study of Malay bomohs at the time. But the Malay bomohs
I was studying were healers, native doctors, some of them
very skilled indeed. Ahmeed did not act or talk like any
bomoh I had met.

Later, I consulted what few books there were about the
aborigines in Malaysia, and talked to people who knew
them. The information I learned was full of specialized
terms, some I had heard and some that were new to me, but
none of the information made sense, and none of it seemed
relevant to what I had experienced in Three. Yes, the Sng'oi
were known to have what perhaps could be called shamans,
or even healers. But none of the descriptions fit what I now
knew of Ahmeed.

All over the world people have shamans, men or women

who, through predisposition and/or training, are guides to the spirit world, as they were described in anthropological books. After Ahmeed's introduction of the Lord of the Great Ocean, it was easy to believe he was such a one.

Weeks later, I asked Ahmeed what the Lord of the Great Ocean looked like.

Ahmeed seemed surprised, thought about it, then said, "Datok Laut Besar is not a person. It is easier to tell people about the Ocean when you can say Datok Laut Besar. No . . . I did not see a person. I find the Great Ocean in my heart."

As we stood around, I about to be on my way home, Ahmeed repeated, with emphasis, "If you were Sng'oi, it would be very simple: you would have learned to become like me. But for a white person . . . we do not know what to do."

Most of the people of Three were now standing around, looking at me with great intensity and, I thought at the time, benevolent expectation. Some of them smiled; all of them stood with their eyes on me, waiting for something.

As always, there was a pause, a moment of silence.

"So," he said, firmly, "we have talked, and what we tell you is this, so that you yourself can decide: If you want, you can learn. If you do not want, we understand."

Yes, all the people nodded, still with that air of expectancy.

It was one of those moments that seem to mark a Y in the road, a node, a point around which the whole universe pivots. I was asked to make a decision that, in my heart, was no longer a decision at all. I cannot remember what I thought. Probably I did not think at all. Decisions as important as this are made intuitively; the mind cannot grasp such choices. I know I did not think what it might mean to be whatever it was Ahmeed was. I had no thought for what the learning might involve in the way of time and commitment. I was intensely aware, however, of the smiles of these people—their warmth, and their expectation.

I knew I was offered a great gift.

Without thinking, I said, "Yes, I want to learn."

Later I realized that Ahmeed never used the word *teach;* he always said *learn.* Looking back, I am certain he saw his role as an opener of doors, never telling me what to do or what to think. What learning I did would be through my own effort—but at the time I did not know that.

Nobody said anything.

I saw only their smiles. I felt elated. I felt loved as I had experienced love but a few times in my life before—perhaps what is called unconditional love. I turned to look at this person, at that person. I smiled until my face ached.

Finally, I turned to Ahmeed and said something inane, like, "Why did you not tell me that you are a bomoh?"

He knew I did not need an answer, so he just smiled.

Learning
to Be Human
Again

I cannot remember when I left, but I got home late in
the afternoon of the same day. Driving home I had realized
that I did not know how to tell my family, my colleagues,
about the extra days away from home and work. What
could I possibly say? I said nothing.

After a few days, absorbed again in my world—in all of
my various realities—the Lord of the Great Ocean became so
strange, so absurdly alien to the way of thinking around me
that I could hardly remember what I had experienced, let
alone talk about my experiences of those days in Three. My
feelings those first few weeks were hidden; I thought I had to
hide them. I did not know how to share what had happened.
I kept a sort of inner glow, fortunately, and at night, in my
dreams, I experienced again the wonders of that evening.

What exactly would I learn? What was Ahmeed, anyway?

I did not have a word for him. Shaman is what I now call
what Ahmeed was. At that time I could think of him only as
a person who was wise, perhaps even psychic. I knew
Ahmeed was not anything like the Malay bomohs I had been

working with, but he obviously had some kind of power.

It would be quite a few years before Carlos Castaneda would publish first one, then a series of books to popularize the idea of shamans. In 1962 I was superficially familiar with some of the anthropological studies on the subject. The word *shaman* comes from Siberia, the texts said, and was used for those who were intermediaries between this world and the spirit world. Shamans were people who healed, who dressed in outrageous costumes, did a sort of trance dance, took toxic substances.

I knew that non-Western peoples around the world had gifted healers and priests with strange powers, but I had no idea what they did.

I grew up in two cultures—more than two, in fact. I had learned two or three languages when I first began to talk, and knew well that you spoke one language to one person and another language to another, and that it was sometimes very difficult, if not impossible, to translate what could be said in one language into another. I was now beginning to realize that the difference among peoples is not a difference of language, but rather of how they experience what is real. That is what is important.

At that time I also thought that *spiritual* meant "religious." I knew, vaguely, that there were people with special qualities, obviously powerful people, but did not think much about them, because they did not fit into my worldview as a Westerner and a scientist.

I remember a strange thing that had happened when I was maybe ten or eleven years old. My father had taken me to the opening of a clinic somewhere in the mountains of Sumatra, where a Tibetan—he might have been from

Nepal, or India, but he was called a Tibetan—did tricks, as my father said. The Tibetan levitated. We all saw that. My father and a few other doctors present looked this way and that, bent over to look under his feet, and discussed what was going on. But on the way back, when I asked my father about it, he used words such as *illusion* and *mass hysteria,* as if it had all been our imagination, as if to say, Do not pay any attention to such things, son.

That is when I learned to be very distrustful of the inexplicable things people did.

After the evening when Ahmeed introduced the Lord of the Great Ocean, however, I remained curious about his descriptions of the ocean. How did he know? How *could* he know?

As happens to people who grow up in two very different worlds, I learned early to be in two different realities. Now, at work or at home with my family, the Lord of the Great Ocean became a story that I did not know what to do with. I tried not to think about it. Ahmeed was simply a charming friend who had accompanied me to Port Dixon. The idea of learning to be whatever he was did not have much reality in my daily life.

But there were other moments—other realities—when Ahmeed and what he had told us of the Lord of the Great Ocean were only too real, and I wanted to be part of that reality; I yearned to be able to *know.*

One time I told the story of the Lord of the Great Ocean to a colleague, someone who I thought had an interest in anthropological material. His interest turned out to be a critique of my methods of fieldwork and my linguistic interpretations of Malay and Sng'oi (neither of which he could speak as well as I). I saw clearly—perhaps for the first time—that most people, even scientists, can see the world only from one point of view: their own.

I went to the library and read what I could find on shamans, healers, and seers. Most books seemed vague, not very specific. A few accounts mentioned substances that made a shaman enter into a trance—this was before the drug culture, before hallucinogens such as LSD and mescaline were talked about and occasionally ingested, though rarely studied. I knew that what had happened in the little hut in Three had nothing to do with mysterious substances. There was no mystery in damar.

Eventually I went back to Three.

Maybe, I thought as I was driving up, it did not happen. Oh yes, when Ahmeed talked about the Lord of the Great Ocean: that really happened. I was certain of that. But I must have imagined talk about learning. Learning what? He did not even have a name for it! As a scientist I knew that naming is the first step, and sometimes the last one, to understanding. When named, we have pigeonholed something, and we think we understand it.

Ahmeed was friendly. All the people in Three were friendly—they had always been friendly.

There were few people that time. I had learned to accept fluctuations in the size of settlements: people were often gone, while others came visiting. One never knew what to expect. We all smiled a great deal, but not a word was said about the Lord of the Great Ocean, or about what had happened the day after Ahmeed's revelation.

In the evening, as we sat around comfortably and cozily,

not saying much, Ahmeed asked me whether I wanted to walk with him the next day. He said it very innocently and casually, making it easy for me to reject or accept.

"Yes, that would be fine," I said, equally casually.

Early the next morning, before the dew had evaporated, we set off. Ahmeed did not seem to have made any preparation. He did not carry anything, so I did not either; I had a few things with me, but left them in Three.

We walked. Neither of us said anything for long periods of time.

As the day progressed, I became hot and sweaty, then thirsty, then hungry. We stopped a few times, sitting on a log or a rock. No mention was made of food or drink, until I told him I was very thirsty. He looked at me, with a sort of grin on his face, and said, "Yes, white people sweat a lot."

He did not sweat at all, it seemed.

Nothing was said about finding water. As we walked on I began to have visions of a coconut tree, climbing—asking *him* to climb—the tree to get a coconut, opening it . . . but we did not carry a parang, and I knew that in any case there are no coconut trees in the jungle.

Finally I asked him to find me something to drink. I was too thirsty. He stopped and cut a little hole in a vine with his thumbnail. I drank the water. It tasted sort of green, but it was clear and clean.

We walked back into Three an hour or so before the sun went down. I wondered whether this aimless silent walking would help me learn . . . whatever it was.

Some people had cooked rice that evening. The People do not always eat rice, nor do they always eat together. Often each person scrounges something to eat during the day. In the evening there is very sweet tea and not much to eat. There were some vegetables that had been cooked with the rice, and some dried fish. I ate heartily. I was hungry and thirsty.

After my second cup of tea, Ahmeed leaned over and took the cup away from me: "We walk tomorrow. Better you not drink." Remembering the vine and the green-tasting water, I assented readily enough. I agreed to walk again the next day. It was enjoyable; I saw things in the jungle that I had not seen before. There was a sense of adventure, of exploring.

The second day went much as the first. We walked, we rested a few times, but we did not eat or drink. I again became tired thirsty, and hungry—but, I admit, not as thirsty or hungry as the day before.

Ahmeed did not volunteer any information. He did not teach. When I asked him something, he barely answered, just grunted something.

We walked all day.

In the evening, back at Three, I asked him what I should learn from these walks. He laughed loudly, which was unusual for him.

"No, I am serious," I protested. "I need to know what it is I should learn."

He chuckled and said, "It does not matter. You do not have to understand; you [will] learn."

I felt abashed. I did not understand his method of teaching. I thought about it all evening, and probably in my sleep as well. In the morning I woke up with the realization that we Westerners are so used to thinking of training, learning, and teaching as verbal activities that we forget that much—perhaps most—learning happens without verbal instruction.

✠ ✠

Unfortunately, I could not stay another day; I had to get back to work, back to my family. I promised Ahmeed I would return as soon as I could, and would make arrangements to stay longer. He looked at me with a smile that said, You people are so strange with your incomprehensible customs, with your thinking and planning—do what you must do.

The next time I could come I stayed several days. I came prepared to learn without verbal instruction. I felt free, curious, ready for whatever I would learn. I had told myself I did not even need to understand what it was I was supposed to learn.

We walked. I learned to go without water and food for seven or eight hours and felt good about myself. Ahmeed never volunteered information. He was friendly. He smiled but did not say much—he did not even answer questions. In the evenings I found I had nothing to say. We ate silently. I fell asleep soon after.

On the third day a sort of uneasiness crept up on me. I was beginning to think of my obligations at home and at work. If I did not *learn* something here, I was wasting my time. I thought I was getting to know what the jungle looked like; I recognized plants, trees, smells, and small sounds from previous walks.

I do not think we walked the same paths—in fact, most of the time there were no paths to follow, but Ahmeed seemed to know where he was going so I followed in his footsteps.

Yes, I definitely was beginning to feel I was wasting my time. I could not take this much time from my work and my family. I had to *do* something, and soon.

When we were resting at the end of the morning, I

looked at Ahmeed and asked him what he thought of me—
was I learning?

He looked at me with astonishment. How could he
know? Only I could know that.

I told him I did not feel any different. In fact, I told him, I
did not get it at all. I did not understand what I was doing here.
I was not learning anything. "Please tell me," I almost begged.

He looked away.

We resumed our walk, which to me had become hard,
tiring, boring work. I was thinking about what I would do
tomorrow—what I would have to do, in fact, to catch up
on things I was supposed to have done today: There was a
meeting I must attend. Oh, and I had forgotten to write my
part of a report, which had been due yesterday. And . . .

When we came back that evening I felt discouraged.
The promise of learning to be whatever Ahmeed was was
not being fulfilled. I was not learning anything. I felt confused, distracted, angry.

Back in the city, my work did not go well. Nothing seemed
to go smoothly. I became ill with a skin disorder, which doctors diagnosed variously as a rash, some kind of dermatitis,
a non-specific this, and a localized that. They did tests, then
gave me cortisone. Nobody told me to taper off the cortisone, so when I stopped the first course, I became sicker.
One of the doctors came up with a diagnosis of "autoimmune reaction." I asked what I might be reacting to.

He said, "Frankly, I do not know. *Autoimmune* essentially means that you are allergic to yourself. As to why, I
could not say. Only you would know that."

There it was again: only I could know. They did not
take responsibility for my health, I thought angrily. I put

my trust in doctors—just as I had sheepishly followed Ahmeed, trusting him to do whatever it was he was supposed to do, and all they could do was throw it back in my face, saying that only I could know.

I was beginning to curse the day I had taken Ahmeed with me to Port Dixon, and the day I had attended that wonderful performance of his. That is all it was, after all, I thought to myself with a sneer, a performance.

Everything felt stuck. I felt miserable and lost. I itched. One of the doctors suggested therapy.

"What kind of therapy," I asked.

"Oh," he said breezily, "maybe you should see Dr. —— [a psychiatrist]." That shocked me. Was that the kind of sickness I had?

My crisis somehow came to an end. Or, more accurately, it faded very slowly. The rash, or whatever it was, eventually disappeared. I went back to work. I picked up some reading that I had neglected during the days (or was it weeks?) I had felt sorry for myself, itching in an air-conditioned bedroom.

During moments when I was honest with myself, I knew that nothing had changed; I was as confused as before. I was still blocked—I vaguely felt there was something I had to learn from "those aborigines," but what it was I did not know. And what was worse, I did not know how to go about learning to learn whatever it was I had to learn.

❈ ❈

A long time passed before I finally went back to Three. I was almost hoping that Ahmeed would not be there. Maybe none of the people I knew would be there and I would not have to explain why I had not come back earlier.

They were all there. Ahmeed seemed genuinely happy to see me. Nobody asked any questions. I had been rehearsing how to explain why I had not come earlier. I had been very sick, I would say, with gory details of doctors and medicines. That was almost the truth: I really had not been *very* sick, but I had been very uncomfortable from being allergic to myself.

However, nobody asked, so I did not need to say anything.

That evening, Ahmeed asked, "Walk tomorrow?"

I answered, "Yes, walk tomorrow."

The morning was especially beautiful, I thought, crisp with a chill in the air. It felt good being out in the jungle again and I was looking forward to the walk.

I made a firm resolve not to have any expectations. Whatever happened would happen. I wanted to have all the wonder a child has at the beginning of a day. We walked. I was thirsty and very tired—I was sadly out of shape after a month of inactivity. In the early afternoon, the hottest part of the day, when it might be cool in the shade but very humid—we came to a big clump of bamboo about twenty feet ahead. Bamboo tends to bunch together, forming an impenetrable barrier.

Ahmeed stopped, listened, turned to me (I was walking behind him), and motioned: *Be silent.*

I opened my mouth to ask a question, but he gestured quite firmly, motioning with his hand: *No talking, stay still, quiet.*

We stood frozen for what seemed a long minute when from the right a large light-colored snake came from under some bushes, slowly crossed in front of us, and passed out of sight into the trees on our left.

Snakes, of course, are everywhere. I had learned long ago to watch out for them, which almost always means looking up in trees. Snakes generally do not crawl on the ground. Large snakes are not common, and a large snake crawling straight across the ground was even more unusual. This snake was large, maybe fourteen or more feet long. It looked as if it had recently eaten something; it moved slowly and seemed fat through the middle. But it moved determinedly, I thought, as if it had a purpose.

I did not try to determine what kind of snake it was, or think much about it. I was too curious about how Ahmeed knew that the snake was there. I was certain he could not have heard anything—the snake made no noise that I could detect. I doubt that Ahmeed could have seen it before it moved out into the open, a few feet in front of us. Did he smell it? Not very likely.

Then how did he know?

We stayed where we were for a few more minutes, all the time Ahmeed making sure that I did not move or make a noise. Then, when we were ready to resume our walk, he again motioned, *slowly, make no noise, no talking.* We turned to our right, walked around the clump of bamboo, and continued on as if nothing had happened.

Maybe half an hour after that, we found a good place to sit down. I was mulling over in my mind how he could have known.

I asked him, "Did you know that snake was coming?"

"Yes," was all he would say.

I tried to phrase the question differently: Had he heard it, seen it?

No, but he knew.

We walked on, my thoughts falling over each other. I

returned to the evening when he had introduced us to the Lord of the Great Ocean. That had been a similar mystery. He had seen the ocean—and only the surface of the ocean at that. He probably had not even put his feet in the water, but he had *known* many things about the ocean that he could not possibly have known.

"When we were in Port Dixon, did you walk into the ocean?" I asked.

No, he confessed, he did not get his feet wet.

"Is the ocean rainwater?" I questioned him, thinking I would trap him.

"Salty," he said.

"But how did you know?" I burst out.

He smiled his childlike smile.

That night I did not sleep well. I realized that I was almost on to something, but I did not know what. Obviously Ahmeed knew things about the environment that I might have learned from what other people told me or from what I read in books. I might even have known that snake was coming if I had modern instruments that were more sensitive than my ears, my nose, or my eyes.

Was Ahmeed more sensitive? Had he trained his senses to be supersensitive?

I had to stay another day, I felt, although my plan was to go back home. I could always leave in the afternoon.

The next day, after walking an hour, I realized that I was thinking so much that I did not pay attention to where we were, to what was going on in the environment. I was trying to figure things out in my head, making lists, weighing probabilities as if Ahmeed's talents were a problem in statistics. I decided instead to really open my ears, my eyes, my nose, my skin to whatever I could pick up in the jungle around us.

I stopped abruptly.

The jungle was suddenly dense with sounds, smells, little puffs of air here and there. I became aware of things I had largely ignored before. It was as if all this time I had been walking with dirty eyeglasses—and then someone washed them for me; or as if I were watching a blurry home movie— and then someone turned the focusing knob. But it was more than that—much more. I could smell things I had no name for. I heard little sounds that could be anything at all. I saw a leaf shivering. I saw a line of insects crawling up a tree.

Ahmeed noticed that I had been walking slower and slower while paying intense attention to the world around me. He too stood still.

"Sit?" he asked.

"Well, no . . . not really . . . perhaps . . . I don't know," I stammered.

"Drink?" he asked.

Afterward I realized that he had spoken very softly, so as not to intrude on what was going on inside me, and he had used simple, single words: Sit? Drink? Yes, I was very thirsty. I looked at him, thinking he would find a water vine. He was the person who knew the jungle, after all. He looked back at me with a perfectly blank expression. He was not helping. He was not talking.

Suddenly, a new thought burst in on me: maybe I could sense water. In my mind I made a sort of list: seeing water, hearing water, smelling water. I might smell water, or even hear it if it was dripping on a leaf perhaps. I looked around.

"Do not talk," Ahmeed said—I knew he meant "Do not think." "Water inside heart," he said next, with a gesture of his hand on his heart. I knew he meant I should sense *inside*—not with my mind, but from the inside.

It is sad to have to use so many words to say something so simple.

As soon as I stopped thinking, planning, deciding, analyzing—using my mind, in short—I felt as if I was pushed in a certain direction. I walked a few steps and immediately saw a big leaf with perhaps half a cup of water in it.

I must have stood there for a full minute, in awe. Not in awe of anything in particular, simply in awe.

When I leaned over to drink from the leaf, I saw water with feathery ripples, I saw a few mosquito larvae wriggling on the surface, I saw the veins of the leaf through the water, some bubbles, a little piece of dirt. Reaching out, I put a finger in the water, then saw that one of the wriggling mosquito larvae had been trapped in a tiny bubble on my finger. How beautiful, how perfect. I did not put the finger with the water droplet in my mouth, but looked back at the leaf.

My perception opened further. I no longer saw water— what I felt with my whole being was a leaf-with-water-in-it, attached to a plant that grew in soil surrounded by uncounted other plants, all part of the same blanket of living things covering the soil, which was also part of a larger living skin around the earth. And nothing was separate; all was one, the same thing: water—leaf—plant—trees—soil— animals—earth—air—sunlight and little wisps of wind. The all-ness was everywhere, and I was part of it.

I cannot explain what went on inside me, but I knew

that I had learned something unbelievably wonderful. I felt more alive than I had ever felt before.

All of me was filled with being.

What this other sense is, I do not know. For me it is very real. I think of it as a sense of *knowing*. It probably is a quality we all have to a greater or lesser degree. For me it works when I can get out of my mind, when I can experience without having to understand, or name, or position, or judge, or categorize.

It is a quality that has to be used or it fades away; just as one has to exercise muscles, so too *knowing* must be exercised.

I am saying this after the fact, trying to describe something that does not fit into our Western concepts, and therefore there are no words. At the time I did not think anything. I was learning how to put my mind aside and use some other sense to know.

Standing over a leaf with a little water in it, somewhere in the jungles of Malaysia, I did not think in words. I did not think. I bathed in that overwhelming sense of oneness. I felt as if a light was lit deep inside me. I knew I was radiating something—love, perhaps—for this incredible world, this rich, varied, and totally interconnected world of creations that, at the same time, gave love to me. And with the love, I also felt a very deep sense of belonging.

✸ ✸

After a while, I slowly woke up. I came to, so to speak, and was in my body again. I looked around. Ahmeed was not where I thought he was. In fact, he was not anywhere in sight. He must have walked on, I thought.

And as soon as I *thought,* I panicked. I realized that I was alone, that Ahmeed had left me in a strange place. I had no idea where I was, or how to get back to Three or to find Ahmeed. My first reaction was to shout, to yell, to call him. But the sense of being part of this wonderful whole was so strong that I could not raise my voice. I opened my mouth and tried to make a sound, but no sound would pass my throat. I could not possibly disturb this oneness by yelling, by feeling panicked. *I could not be afraid*—after all, I was part of this all-ness.

My life changed in that moment.

And then I knew I need not shout for help, I need not run after Ahmeed. I knew with a great certainty that all I had to do was put my mind aside and *know* where he was. Almost immediately I *knew:* He was not too far away. I had an impression of him walking leisurely in *that* direction. He sauntered as if he were deep in thought, or perhaps he was thinking of me. In my mindless state of being I sent him a voiceless hello, and it was easy to imagine receiving his slight smile that barely stretched the corners of his mouth.

Part of me wanted to join Ahmeed, go back to Three to eat and drink. But another part wanted to stay here and know this new world more intimately. I stayed.

I was certain I would find my way back to Ahmeed and the village later, when it grew dark perhaps.

I have no idea how long I stayed—there is no time in that mindless state—but it was quite dark when I finally returned to the settlement.

When it was time to leave the place where I had discovered the leaf with water (I never drank any, by the way;

I was not thirsty anymore), I extended my knowing to sense where the settlement was. *There,* my knowing told me immediately.

With my new and now extended knowing I became aware of a soft sound, some distance away. At first I did not recognize the sound. It seemed familiar, but I had no name for it and in that state I avoided naming, understanding, and recognizing. But this sound wanted to be acknowledged. It intruded on my being, almost as if introducing itself: I am Tiger. It was that sound between purring and growling that tigers make when they are not sleeping and not hunting. I think of it as an announcement: I am here. All animals that talk have their own sounds to let the world know *I am here.*

I felt a whisper of fear, but that was a learned reaction, I knew. From earliest childhood I have had a special feeling for tigers. What fear I had of them was the fear others had tried to give me.

Growing up in Sumatra I had seen tigers in the wild several times. The first time was when I was perhaps eight or nine, as we rode in our open-top car. The tiger was in the road in front of us as we came very slowly around a steep, hairpin curve. The driver—my friend Udin—stopped the car. He sat calmly in the driver's seat and I sat beside him. We waited. The tiger certainly must have smelled us. It was night and the headlights had been on, but Udin switched them off. There was enough moonlight to see clearly—the tiger's tail moved rhythmically from side to side. He stood in the middle of the road, his head turned to look at us. He was large, as large as our car, it seemed—his head was at the same level as ours. I do not know how long we sat there, but it felt as if time was suspended; we looked at the tiger and he at us for an eternity.

Finally, the tiger slowly, very slowly, straightened his head in the direction he had been going and softly stepped back into the jungle at the side of the road. As he moved away I heard that soft, growling purr and knew that meant *I am Tiger; I am here.*

Udin waited a few minutes, turned the lights on again, and drove. He looked at me, and said: "'Rimau, tiger," as if to say, Now you know what a tiger is.

When I stood alone in another jungle in Malaysia, listening again to that soft, growling purr, I thought of that first tiger. If I had not been open to the world, I might not have heard the sound at all—it came from far away. Alone this time, I experienced the sound as very comforting.

I knew where Three was, and how to get there. It was not in the direction of the tiger, nor was it away from him. I started walking, still drinking deeply of that wonderful sense of belonging. I was part of this jungle, and the jungle was part of me. The smells, the rich colors now darkening, the sounds of animals were almost overwhelming. The only way I could deal with so much was to feel it as a whole, one—not analyzing, interpreting, naming, sorting, judging.

At times I felt as if I did not even walk; I was flowing through this medium that was everything and also myself.

Darkness falls quickly in the tropics; it was quite dark before I reached Three. I did not hurry. I knew all the time where Ahmeed was—to the side and slightly ahead of me— and all the way back to Three I heard the soft tiger sound traveling with me.

I had a fantasy about that tiger sound: first I thought of it as *Welcome,* as if the tiger were talking to *me,* rather than simply announcing his presence to the world around him perhaps a mile away. Then I imagined the tiger saying to me, *"You are doing well."*

I felt he was as aware of me as I was of him. He walked with me.

Before I reached Three, I had a whiff of the smell of the oil used in the lamps people had lit.

Ahmeed joined me just outside the settlement. Neither of us said anything. We only looked at each other and smiled. I felt my heart swell with pride, with gratitude, with accomplishment, and with other feelings I still do not have words for.

I wish I could recapture the smiles of the Sng'oi. Their smiles were not like ours; they did not show teeth. Sng'oi smiled with their eyes more than their lips. Their eyes lit up. Ahmeed's smile lit up the night as we stepped into the clearing of Three.

I was full of my new knowing. I felt such love for these people—my family, as the trees also were my family, and the grass, and the scruffy dog that ran between our legs, and even the mosquitoes: We were one whole.

The night seemed to be particularly rich with sounds that evening, and sounds, too, were part of all.

I listened for the sound of Tiger, but he had gone.

We ate a meal that someone had cooked. The food tasted incredibly wonderful. There were roots, I remember, that I had not had before, that tasted like . . . bitter sweet potatoes? A few wilted, unnamed vegetables tasted like gourmet spinach. The sugary tea was ambrosia.

After the meal nobody said much, but as I began to be more aware of individual people, I noticed that they were watching me. They knew.

As people were getting ready to go to sleep—the few

dishes they had were wiped and put away, the rice pot was washed in the stream and put away—Ahmeed stood up, and asked me whether I was tired. No, I was wide awake.

"We walk a little," he said.

In the dark people stay close to home. We moved away only a short distance from where the few huts were. We did not sit down (you are careful where you sit down in the dark).

After a long silence, Ahmeed said,

"So . . . you found water."

Yes, I had found water. I had found a whole new world, in fact. I opened my mouth to tell him about what I had felt, experienced. I wanted to tell him that I was finally learning the marvel of being one with the world. But nothing came out of my mouth. I did not have words to say what I wanted to say in English, let alone in Malay, and certainly not in Sng'oi.

I knew that he knew. There was no need for words. Instead, I reached out my hand and touched his elbow. We stood like that for some minutes, communicating without saying a word.

Finally he stepped back a little and said, not looking at me: "Who brought you back?"

He did not ask how I found the way back, but who brought me back.

Without hesitation I said, "Tiger, 'rimau."

I was surprised myself at what I said, but as I said it I realized that it was true. It had been that comforting growling purr of the tiger that had brought me back.

Ahmeed nodded. He repeated, "Harimau."

The Malay word for tiger is *harimau,* usually pronounced *'rimau* — to say *harimau* makes it more formal, more important.

Nothing more was said, and we drifted back to the little huts.

It took me quite a while to come back down, after that day. Everything I did was blessed. Things flowed smoothly.

Because I had spent so much time away, I had to catch up on my work. There were trips to make, research reports to be written. I spent time with my family. I knew I did everything that was expected of me—everything that I had committed myself to do—and yet I also knew that I was not the same person.

I had frequent flashes of what I then called *oneness,* that magical sense of being one with literally everything in creation. Each time I had the oneness experience, it became more natural, more a part of me—not something that I knew, but something I *am.*

✾ ✾

A few years earlier, I had spent a summer in Denmark, sailing with three Danes. We were in our early twenties. They spoke English for my benefit—except when something needed to be communicated in a hurry, as when we were coming into a harbor, for instance. The captain then would yell commands in Danish, and everyone would run to do this and that. I felt completely left out; I did not understand a single word they were saying.

My bunk was stuck away in one of the angles of the boat. As I lay awake at night, in my mind I heard Danish, but it was all one blur. In my frustration I could not distinguish individual words; all I could hear were pure sound, intonation, and rhythm.

The next time we came into a harbor, the same thing happened. Much activity, people running around, commands and comments I didn't understand thrown back and forth in Danish. I hid in the cabin below the deck. When the boat was tied up, they all came down, still excitedly talking Danish among themselves until they saw me—then they switched to English.

Suddenly, out of the blue, I blurted out, among other, less polite words: "Dammit, I cannot understand a word you are saying!"

I was furious, frustrated, angry—and somehow that anger broke through a barrier: suddenly their speech was no longer a string of weird sounds. I could hear words, expressions. On that day I began to learn Danish, and a few days later I had learned enough so that they could send me to a little store to buy supplies—tomatoes, I remember, whose pronunciation in Danish is particularly strange and difficult.

Learning to experience the oneness was very much like learning to hear Danish. I had to break through a veil, a barrier.

I forgot Danish because I did not use it, but after having once experienced the oneness, I can find it again, and each time it becomes easier to slip into that way of being. At first, each time I experienced it I also heard the soft tiger sound, but eventually that faded. I knew the two were separate phenomena. Tiger is with me all the time, and I know that he always has been. Experiencing the oneness, the knowing, was new. It had changed my life.

❈ ❈

It was at least a month before I had an opportunity to go back to Three. I wanted very much to ask Ahmeed questions, to learn how to handle this new knowing.

I should have known that Ahmeed did not teach that way. I asked him to explain, but he did not answer. He did not even let me finish my sentence.

"Let's walk," he said.

We walked.

We did not go far before we sat down on a rock. The air smelled wonderful—I took deep breaths, turned my head this way and that, closed my eyes, and again felt the rich oneness all around me.

This time Ahmeed talked. He told a long story about how he had learned what I had just learned when he was a young boy, perhaps eight or nine years old. A woman had taught him, a woman from another family (another settlement). She came over for a visit and found him sitting by himself with his eyes closed. She hunkered down beside him, and after a while she asked him what he saw.

"Everything, everything . . . ," he had answered.

She took him to her settlement, where he lived with her for many years. During that time she showed him that there were times when it was good to see everything but other times when it was not good. Here Ahmeed looked at me for emphasis: "There are times when it is not good to see everything."

He told me stories of times when he had seen things before they happened, and how frightened he had been at first. He told me stories of strangers who had come to the settlement who did not know who he was and had "talked loud" to him. In Malay culture and also in Sng'oi culture, loud speech, loud noises, as well as strong gestures are considered rude, uncouth, foreign. But he did not mind, he said, he just "shut off seeing."

Again he turned to me for emphasis: "Do you turn off the seeing?"

Yes, I told him, I had to. The people around me would

not understand, so I had to learn that very early.

"Good," he said. Then he added something that I realized only later was very insightful. "You are alone," he said. "It will be difficult for you to see because you do not have the village around you." He used the word *kampong*, suggesting not only a settlement, but especially the extended social relationships of a village, or a Sng'oi settlement.

Now, so many years later, I know what he meant. It is indeed difficult to *know* without the protection of a village or an extended family. I knew that Ahmeed could not help me after I left Malaysia and continued my life elsewhere, but he had been aware of what it must be like for me. He cared.

Ahmeed had been talking for at least half an hour—unusual for him. When he paused I thought he was done. I moved to stand up but he put his hand on my arm, as if to say, No, not yet. Nothing was said for several minutes, but I knew what he was saying to me—not in words, not even in images. I sensed warm, supporting energy coming from him to me.

After a while he said, turning full face to me, "Strong." Be strong!

We both got up to stretch and walk around a bit. I knew we would continue, but Ahmeed had finished one part of what he wanted to share with me. We needed a break before going on. He told me some news about Three. Someone had had a baby, but the baby was born too quickly, and so she did not live. Another woman was pregnant.

"Strange," he said, "two babies in a row. Very unusual."

He asked about my family. This was intermission, social time. We chatted about people, about things that had happened, about daily life.

As we sat down again he continued in a different tone

of voice. It seemed, deeper, almost like the voice he had used when he was in trance.

"Harimau," he began, and then paused for a long time. "Tiger . . . "

For him, he said finally, the animal that helped him was Snake. "We [Sng'oi] do not talk about that," he added. "We never talk about that." Then he said, "Snake show itself."

Large snakes will not cross a path in broad daylight. The snake we had seen that day had shown itself for Ahmeed's sake (and, indirectly, to help me see). I knew he meant to say that the snake had shown itself because Snake is the animal-that-helps-him: if he had not been there with me, the snake would not have been there.

"That knowing is in my heart," he said. The knowledge that Snake is his helper is inside of him, locked up in his heart, his alone. He was sharing something with me that he would not share with anyone else. "That evening, after we eat we walked a little ways so that others would not hear about your Harimau."

Now I understood. He meant to tell me that I could not share my feeling for Tiger with anyone. Tiger is the animal-that-helps-me, and that knowing is in my heart. I should not talk about it.

I had questions. I wanted to ask, Why? But I stopped myself in time. I would have to learn by myself. There would be opportunities later to talk—another time, different circumstances. This evening was too full of meaning to spoil it by asking questions. He had not talked during what I thought of as my training. Now he talked and I would not break the flow.

It was very dark outside and stars were glittering overhead. There was no moon. He shivered a little, not because he was cold, I think, but because of the solemnity of the moment. At last he turned to face me, relaxing his body, as if to say, The ceremony is over.

He said again, "You are alone."

Yes, I was alone with my newfound knowing, without a society or a culture to support me. Then again he added, "Strong."

I thought of a coach telling a player who is walking to the field, "You can do it."

This had been my Initiation, a solemn occasion, even though it was not a public event. I felt as if he had passed on some ancient knowledge. I was intensely grateful for what he had given me, and just as grateful for how he had given it: I learned what *learning* is.

✸ ✸

Over the years my sense of knowing I am a part of this world became stronger; it became a lifeline. It made me feel safe.

I have a strong connection with trees, and through trees I am connected to all the natural world. Trees have become for me a sort of anchor to the natural world. I am energized by them as other people feel energized by rocks or by the ocean. When I stand with my back pressed against an old evergreen, I feel its energy coursing up my spine. That is not a mystical experience; it as a way for me to reconnect with the natural world of which I am a part—it is an affirmation of my humanity.

I never knew whether I had learned what Ahmeed knew. I am not even certain that what I call *knowing* is what Ahmeed calls *seeing*. I do know that Ahmeed helped me regain a sense that being human is being part of the natural world; it is a sense of belonging that all the Sng'oi and many other people have, but that Western people seem to have lost.

Ahmeed knew I lived in a different world, that knowing what he knew would be different for me.

He gave me his support and his blessings.

Privacy and Alienation

One of the questions I did not ask at the end of my training was why it is important to keep from others the knowledge of my animal-that-helps. Why could I not share that? Why should others not know?

An answer to that unasked question came some years later, when I spent a few weeks with other so-called primitive people on a small Pacific island.

People living in a close-knit group, where everyone is family (although not necessarily related by blood), have no privacy. What privacy there can be must be inside one's heart. In such a society people cherish immaterial things that are uniquely personal. For some, one's true name is private. The name one uses in public is just a social convenience. One's real name nobody knows, except perhaps the priest.

Nothing is more cherished, and sometimes private, than what Native Americans call one's totem animal, the animal-that-helps of the Sng'oi.

Westerners have written about the fear native peoples had of being photographed. Explorers explained that the natives were afraid that with the photographic likeness the soul of a person was stolen.

Perhaps taking a picture is an invasion of privacy.

Our society thinks of privacy differently. To us, privacy is space—fenced space. Americans dream of owning their own home on their own piece of land, surrounded by a white picket fence—today perhaps an electrified steel link fence with a sophisticated alarm system. We have created legal fences too, boundaries set down in law: so far and no farther, you cannot say this and that to me, you cannot do this and that in my presence. And woe to those who trespass our many boundaries! Today one is likely to be shot.

In an American home people have their own bedrooms, their own beds, and, if they are rich enough, their own bathrooms and their own cars. Even our bodies have boundaries—we do not touch each other, because touching means something sexual is intended. We have more private *physical* space than anyone in the history of mankind has had.

Yet we are also more alienated from each other—as we are from the earth that nurtures us—than anyone in the history of mankind.

✳ ✳

Today I no longer wonder at the things I say when I let my inner knowing speak. My mouth may surprise me, but when, after I say the words, their meaning penetrates my consciousness, my consciousness admits that my mouth spoke truth.

The knowing I learned is not the same as consciousness. It is far deeper. I have found that sometimes I know something that I cannot possibly know, much as Ahmeed knew about the ocean. That kind of knowing does not fit into the

Western view of what is real. Scientists need to measure, dissect, analyze, and prove harmless before they can accept that a plant has valuable properties, for instance—and, of course, the properties of the plant have to fit into current theories of Western medicine.

Anthropologists and other scientists have occasionally, and with great reluctance, studied herbs that people in out-of-the way places have used for millennia, forgetting that a healing system is just that: A system. Pharmaceuticals cannot be considered separate from the healing system in which they were developed.

Western scientists seem surprised when they find that some herbs and potions work. The next step then is always an elaborate, high-tech chemical analysis of the herb to identify the *active principle*. The active principle is then re-created from chemicals so that it can be commercially produced without the many "impurities" of the original plant material (although now nobody will ever know whether perhaps one or more of those impurities plays an important part in the effectiveness of the natural herb).

The sap of the leaves of aloe vera, for instance, soothes and even heals burns with amazing efficacy, as any who have used it will tell you. There is little profit in selling aloe vera plants, however. But when scientists identified what they named *aloantin* as the active principle, a product could be manufactured and sold commercially.

The explanation Western scientists give for how people all over the world discovered the healing qualities of plants without the benefit of our sophisticated science is always the same: trial and error—as if primitive people tried this tree bark, or that leaf, and perhaps experimented with cooking it, eating it raw, shredding it, baking it until, in the end, they kept what worked.

In reality, the preparation of many native foods and medicines is often so complicated, requiring so many steps, that it is hard to imagine how people would use trial and error to learn what is good and safe to eat, or which herbs prepared which ways prove to be medicinal.

How would people discover through trial and error that *curare*, a quick and deadly poison that can be applied to blow darts or arrows, must be prepared by collecting the sap of the plant and cooking it down to a thick paste, being careful, the whole time, not to touch it with their hands? (Touching often means ingesting, for those who do not frequently wash their hands.)

In some parts of the world the staple food is made from a root vegetable (*cassaba,* in South America) that contains very toxic prussic acid. The root must be washed, peeled, shredded, soaked in water, wrung out (using great pressure), washed and squeezed again, dried to a powder, then mixed with water and cooked. All those steps through trial and error? One wonders how many thousands of people must have died from trying the wrong thing, or the wrong sequence of steps in the preparation.

Did people discover edible mushrooms through trial and error?

All through history there have been people who knew with an inner knowing.

Once, while walking up the steep and very narrow trail that goes into Hanakapi'ai Valley on the island of Kaua'i, I had an almost disabling sinus headache. Each step pounded in my head. As I trudged up the steep trail, I looked up and saw a plant I did not know, maybe twenty feet above me on the side of the cliff. As I looked at the plant, I knew what it would feel like (hairy, but not stinging), what it would smell like (aromatic), and I knew that if I could get even one leaf of that plant, crush it, and put it in my nose, it would clear my sinuses. A friend reached up with a long stick and managed to break off a leaf of the plant. It felt as I knew it would, and it smelled as I knew it would. I put it in my nose. It cleared my sinuses, as I knew it would.

The plant, I later learned, is a wild species of oregano. Hawaiians know it for its medicinal properties.

Another time, in the mountains of Luzon in the Philippines, walking from one Igorod village to the next with two Igorod guides, I slipped perhaps thirty feet down a very steep slope of scree and badly scraped the insides of both hands. I knew that I had better not get an infection on the inside of my hands: We were at least two days from civilization. I looked for water, but the landscape was dry and sere and there was no water near us. I saw a plant that grew all around, and again I knew what the leaf of that plant would feel like (hard, harsh, prickly), what it would taste like if I chewed it (bitter). The knowing came in a set. I also knew what to do with these leaves: I had to chew them to make a poultice that would clean out the dirt from the many scrapes on my hands and perhaps even disinfect the wounds.

I chewed the leaves, wrapped the poultice with some other leaves, and tied the ungainly bundle to my hands with vines. In the evening, when we reached the village where we would stay the night, I opened the bandages and found that the wounds were clean and without infection.

The same plant grows in Hawaiʻi, and, of course,

Hawaiians also know it as a medicinal plant (it is of the verbena family).

To me, this knowing is real; it is a fact as much as seeing is a fact, or that being left-handed is real. There are times when I wish I could turn off this knowing. But humans are not like machines; it is not easy to turn off the senses—nor is it easy to turn them on.

When we moved to Hawai'i, after two years in Malaysia, I went through a long period of adjustment. The kind of openness I had learned with the Sng'oi probably has survival value in a tropical jungle, but in the jungle of a modern city it is a burden.

I learned that I did not want to sense what people were feeling. It was frightening to discover how many people think nothing at all, but *feel* waves of anger, resentment, and bitterness—although they act as if they are deaf and blind to their own feelings. Often our environments are so full, so busy, that allowing all senses (including the knowing sense) to be open will result in overload.

I am certain I am not the only one who has to turn off some senses in a supermarket, or in a train station or airport. I avoid these places of howling overload if at all possible. One learns—*has* to learn—to shut off some senses, to protect oneself from all that noise.

What Do
Those Hundred
Men Do?

O ne day I went to a Sng'oi settlement deep in the mountains, a few hours' walk through the jungle. It was quite late when I reached the settlement. As usual, someone was waiting along the side of the path when I arrived—a young woman this time who, as had others, silently stood up and walked ahead to the little village.

In the evening, when we sat around getting acquainted, someone asked, "Did you pass by that place where they are making a new road?"

Yes, indeed, that was the way I had come. That is, in fact, why it got so late; the men who worked there had to clear a path so that my car could pass.

"Is it true," someone else asked, "that there is a machine there that does the work of a hundred men?"

I must have felt a sense of pride in our cleverness, our inventiveness, our machines. A machine that does the work of a hundred men—that well describes a bulldozer.

"Yes," I said, "there is such a machine there."

Long silence.

Then another person spoke up: "What do those hundred men do?"

It was my turn to be silent. I had never considered labor-saving devices from that point of view. What did those hundred people do who were displaced by one bulldozer? I did not know.

Today, the children of those hundred men probably work in an office, or they make shoes. Perhaps they made the computer I am working on now. It seems inevitable that machines will take over—or have taken over already—much of the labor that was done by people not too long ago.

We do not think much about what those hundred men do.

I did not know what to say. I had not thought about the hundred men. The ebb and flow of the gentle conversation around a tiny fire moved on to other subjects. We talked about a mysterious sickness, I remember, that had come to a neighboring settlement.

But the thought of those hundred men now out of work haunts me still.

What do those hundred men do?

✵ ✵

Not long after that I visited a Malay kampong. Malays are far from primitive; they accept many of the things of modern technology, although not Western culture itself. The Malay culture is coherent, complex, and complete, and is very much part of everyone's life.

Every place has its own uniqueness, but this village at first seemed so typical, so average that it was bland. Not much was going on when the driver and I arrived, shortly after midday. The houses looked much as one would expect in this part of the country: Neglected, in need of repair, but not really decrepit yet. A few people were lounging around dreamily. A handful of children, half asleep on the fringes of the little group of adults, sat or lay in the dirt. Nobody showed any interest in us or even looked at us with curiosity as we came closer. No one came to greet us or to check us out. None of the children seemed awake or alert enough even to stare, as children will.

My driver and I were absorbed in the village's lethargy. I felt as if we were moving through thick molasses as we approached what looked like the hanging-out place, located—of course—under a big tree, the coolest spot at this time of day.

We silently merged into midday village life: hanging out, doing nothing. We mumbled some greeting. It was peaceful, certainly. It was too hot for mosquitoes—they would come later. Flies were not flying. There was no breeze—not a leaf was twitching. Even the spirits had gone elsewhere.

An hour or so later it began to feel cooler. A few children began to fuss. They disappeared to go their own mysterious ways. A middle-aged man next to me looked up, awake enough to ask where we came from. No one would ask what we were doing in the village. That was not the way of Malays, but it was polite to inquire where we were from. And slowly, very slowly, a conversation grew.

By pleasantly cool midafternoon, most of the village stood around us. We had explained where we were from, and in the process mentioned who we were. Now it would be their turn to tell us about themselves.

First, however, someone wanted to know the latest gossip from the capital. Was it true that a famous politician had an affair with an even more famous movie star? I had a friend who goes to the kind of parties where politicians, famous movie stars, and foreigners mix, but even he would not have known whether that was just rumor—and nasty gossip at that—or whether there was truth to the story. Was it true, someone else asked, that the prime minister had gone on an extended visit to Europe, and would visit the queen? Yes, we assured them, that was definitely true. In fact, the PM had already met with the queen; the story, with their picture, was in all the papers this morning.

A sigh of wonder wafted over the group: *wahhhh!*

There almost certainly was at least one transistor radio in this village. A few people here probably could read the papers, but it would take a few days for newspapers to reach them. This was a poor village, off the beaten track, but they knew what was happening in the capital.

Few of the villagers were wearing traditional dress, although all of them wore sarongs, faded and threadbare as they might be. But there were also nylon shirts, some watches, even costume jewelry, and a hat that looked as if it had gone through at least one war.

There was not much to tell about the village, it seemed. They were just ordinary people—not much happened here. The only thing that might be different in this village was that an inventor lived here! Someone had invented a machine, they told us—and he lives right in the village. They said the word in English: *mah-tcheen*, adding a *t* to make the word sound more explosive, more aggressive.

There were probably not more than fifteen adults standing around, and I could not imagine any of them having invented a machine.

"No," a woman who stood at the back said, "he is not here, he does not leave his house very often. He is a recluse."

Another voice added, ". . . and he cannot hear, nor can he talk."

We all moved to visit this inventor who was a recluse and a deaf-mute. He lived in what was almost certainly the smallest and shabbiest house in the village. His wife met us, standing in front of the door to make clear that we were not welcome inside. The house was so small that we probably could not have stood up inside. She motioned for us to go next door to a small, barnlike structure. She was not deaf and she could speak, we learned later, but perhaps living with a deaf-mute husband had made her silent as well.

It was getting close to sunset and what light came into the barn came through the door and a few chinks in the walls. In the gloom we saw a structure of heavy beams and pulleys. The inventor stood aside to let us in, eyes downcast. He was a slight man, unusually thin even for someone in a poor village, as if he had been hungry for a long time.

He quickly motioned to his wife, and made some signs to a few of the women who were edging into the small space. Some of the women left.

I could not imagine what the machine would do, but it looked competent—strong, simple, almost new. The wood had not discolored yet, although in places it had worn smooth or perhaps had been polished.

The place was dark and parts of the machinery were behind a partition. When I studied the machine I saw pulleys, stout *sennit* (coconut fiber) ropes connecting a heavy beam of wood to heavy bamboo supports. I still could not imagine what the machine would do or what it was for. By

now most of the villagers had come and were standing outside, waiting for the show to begin.

There was some mumbling and a bit of confusion when
the inventor gave more hand signs and a few more women
disappeared. Maybe ten minutes later—it was dark now;
little oil lamps had been brought to light up the inside of
the barn—the women returned, single file, each with a
handful of unhulled rice.

Now I understood what the machine would do. The
inventor had invented a mill!

Traditionally, each household hulls rice once a day.
Without refrigeration food does not keep well in the hot,
humid tropics. Raw, unhulled rice keeps better than rice
that is hulled and ready to cook. A block of wood with a
cup-shaped depression holds some unhulled rice; the pestle is a long wooden pole that pounds the hulls off the rice.
Two, sometimes three women (or girls) take turns lifting
the pole and letting it fall into the mortar, sometimes with
some force. It is an ancient ritual; the movements of lifting and dropping are done with the whole body. Pounding
rice looks almost like a dance. The pestle bonging into the
mortar makes a wonderfully syncopated rhythm that fits
the dance of the women, who often sing to accompany
themselves. They obviously did not dislike this work—
they usually smiled and laughed while lifting and letting
fall the long pole.

I had thought of it as woman's work—just as getting
water from the river, or from a standpipe, was woman's
work, accompanied by much giggling and gossip sharing.

The mortar in the barn was considerably larger than
those used by a household; the depression might hold as
much as six or seven cups of rice. The pestle was the large

beam I had seen sticking up into the dark recesses under the roof; its bottom end was rounded and smooth, and thicker and much heavier than the poles used for one household.

The inventor stepped on a treadle and slowly the machine came to life. It took a few minutes to get the pestle to move up and fall down, but when its rhythm had been established, it became clear that one rather scrawny man could hull, in a few minutes, all the rice five or six families would need for a meal.

The demonstration lasted no longer than five minutes. The inventor proudly showed us a small bucketful of smoothly hulled rice, visibly cleaner, smoother, and whiter than ordinary village rice. I knew that it would take five or six households half an hour to hull that much rice, yet this had been hulled in a few minutes.

The onlookers waited for our comments. We oohed and aahed and exclaimed what a wonderful machine this was— wondering meanwhile why it was so obviously unused. The villagers were proud of the inventor in their midst but they did not use his invention.

Here was genuine native genius at work: a laborsaving device invented by a simple, almost certainly illiterate villager. Even from this simple demonstration it was clear that this slight man could easily have hulled all the rice needed each day for the whole village in less than half an hour a day. That would leave all the women and girls who now did their daily rice-pounding dance with nothing to do but . . .

Obviously the women did not think of hulling rice as a chore, as hard or unpleasant work. Perhaps it was something they looked forward to doing. It was part of the daily rhythm of life.

Nobody in the village seemed to work hard, or to work long hours—except perhaps during the short, intense days of planting and harvesting rice. The activities that kept the people in this village alive—getting firewood for a little cooking, hulling rice, planting, tending the rice fields, fishing occasionally, growing some vegetables—all these were not thought of as work; it was what they did each day. Together these activities made the rhythm of their lives, a pleasant routine, essentially unchanged for many generations. They felt no need to change.

As we walked outside I asked the inventor's wife whether the inventor had seen pictures of a similar machine in a book. She obviously did not know what I was talking about. I doubted that she or he had ever seen a book with schematic drawings of anything like that mill. So I asked her how he had thought of making his machine. She paused for a moment, then she went inside the little house and came back with two handfuls of crude models made of pieces of bamboo, twigs, and string, each mounted on a piece of cardboard.

The inventor had invented by making and trying out scaled-down models; he had discovered the principle of moving a large upright beam with a small force. The models looked childishly crude compared to the finished product. It was hard to imagine that the models would work. But the finished product certainly did.

It was quite dark as we walked back to the car, followed by the adults and many of the children. They asked again how we liked the demonstration. Was this not a wonderful invention? Yes, we agreed, it was indeed a wonderful invention. The fact that it was not used obviously did not lessen its value to them. The villagers perhaps thought of the inventor and his invention as we might think of an artist and his art: not useful, but something to be proud of, something we might display in a museum.

One day we may put our bulldozers in museums.

We Take Care of Each Other

Shortly before leaving Malaysia I was asked to meet with a visiting psychologist. He had been told to talk with me, he said. Perhaps I could explain something that baffled him.

He had been taken to see one of the two mental hospitals in Malaysia and had been told that there was not a single Malay patient. There were a large number of Chinese, a few Indians (from India, Pakistan, or Ceylon—but all of them were referred to as Indian at that time), perhaps even a few white people. But no Malays.

"When Malays make up half the population of this country," he said with anger in his voice, "then it is impossible that there would be no mentally ill Malays. And what makes it all even more unacceptable," he added, "is that in the other mental hospital it is the same: no Malays. What is going on?" he wanted to know.

From his manner I could tell that he was almost convinced there was some sort of conspiracy. From his point of view it was impossible, unthinkable, that a population of several million people did not have any crazy people, angry people, dangerous people who should be locked away in mental hospitals.

I suggested we visit some Malay villages.

By that time I knew the country fairly well. I had visited many Malay villages and I knew where we would be welcomed, where we could easily talk with people. I doubt that there is any culture, anywhere, that does not have a certain amount of shyness about letting strangers in on their most frightening psychological conditions. Mental illness is not something you can discuss easily on a first visit. But I felt certain that the villagers I knew would be willing at least to talk with us.

The same driver who had taken me around many times before agreed to drive us. The visitor and I sat in the back, talking psychology. He said he had heard that I had made a "sort of study" of the Malays. Yes, but my study was really about dietary behavior, and my own interest was in healing systems, healers, and the many issues around what we call medical services. But I felt I knew the Malays fairly well— after all, I grew up a few hundred miles from here among other Malays in Indonesia. And yes, I was a psychologist.

We discussed at length what I thought were the central values of Malay culture. I remember trying to explain the words *halus* and *kasar*.

"*Kasar* means crude, rough, loud, insensitive—"

"And," the driver added, "thick, curly, or kinky hair, the kind of hair that feels like steel wool."

I continued: "*Halus* means soft, gentle, polite—"

Here the driver turned back again, and with a smile added, "It also means soft straight hair: Malay hair."

"Halus," I said, "is what the culture says all Malays are or should be. Kasar is what foreigners are—loud Chinese, ruthless white people, crude Indians."

Once more the driver turned around. He asked me, "What about the Orang Asli, the aborigines? They sometimes have curly or even kinky hair. Are they kasar?"

"You know very well they are the essence of halus," I could not help saying.

"Yes," he mused, "that is true. Maybe that means they are the old Malays. Do you think that is possible?"

There was indeed one group of aborigines whom anthropologists and government officials called proto-Malays, supposedly the stock from which Malays evolved. The Sng'oi, the only group of aborigines I knew, had sometimes intermarried with Malays, but they had a different culture, although in this case they certainly had similar values.

It was true that Malays were told from earliest childhood that to be Malay is to be halus. Malays did not raise their voices, they—

The driver could not help another interruption. "Yes," he said, "that is true in the kampong. But in the city it is getting very difficult to be Malay, when all around you there are *kafirs* [unbelievers] who are kasar."

I hope the visitor could sort out our discussion, which was held in Malay with the driver and in English with the visitor.

We visited two villages that first day, spending time being introduced to the head of the village, to some of the elders, as the visitor called them—the older people who happened to be around. We walked here and there. We talked with children. We admired their rice fields. We were served sweet tea in the community shelter of one village, very sweet lemonade in the next.

The visitor asked some pointed questions, but no, nobody had ever heard of a person who had been crazy, or dangerous, or mentally ill.

The next day we visited three villages, the last one quite far away; we did a lot of driving that day. The second village, however, began to provide an answer to the question the visitor had asked.

It was the middle of the day, the time when nobody moves, let alone works, if it can be avoided. We stood around under a large tree, trying to catch a little breeze. Our discussion with the elders was leisurely and vague.

From the corner of my eye I saw someone flitting from one tree to another, obviously trying to hide. I looked again but did not see anything more. Then again I saw someone— a man, I thought—flitting from one hiding place to another.

The visitor, too, had noticed. We asked why anyone, at this time of day, would run from one hiding place to another. Whom was he hiding from?

"Oh," someone said, quite nonchalantly, "that is our thief."

We said, "Your thief?"

"Yes, he likes to steal things."

"Did you call the police?"

"No, of course not. Why should we? He is one of us, he lives in this kampong." And that was the end of the discussion.

A week later the visitor joined us again for a last trip to a village even farther away. This time as soon as we arrived we were dogged by an old woman, bent with age but spry and very active—almost hyperactive. She had strange mannerisms, she mumbled, and every now and then she would scream out what sounded like curses. Then she would shuffle closer to us and cackle like a madwoman.

Nobody in the village took much notice of her, except once, when she wanted to touch the visitor's camera. One of the men called her by name, took her elbow, and said, "Come now, grandma, do not bother us, we are talking."

She wandered away, mumbling, screeching every now and then, until she disappeared and we could not hear her anymore.

The visitor asked what was wrong with the woman. Oh, nothing, everyone assured us. That is just what she does. It does not bother anyone.

It would not occur to Malays to have this woman committed to a mental hospital. After all, she is part of the village: She is one of us.

Nor would it occur to Malays to have the police come to take a thief away: He too is one of us.

That was why there were no Malays in the two mental hospitals.

How about violent behavior? the visitor wanted to know. Are there not dangerous people in your kampongs? No, no, everyone was quite sure that there were no dangerous people.

"How about that woman?" he persisted. "She yells and curses—does not she sometimes strike out at someone?"

It is difficult to phrase a conditional sentence in Malay, but even with a great deal of explaining, the people in this kampong were quite sure that this woman had never struck out at anyone.

"Not even a dog?" the visitor wanted to know.

No, not even a dog.

Driving back the visitor grumbled; he was sure they and we were hiding something. There must be violence, he said. Maybe not often, but sometimes.

I mentioned that the only cultural expression of violence in Malay culture is *amok,* a word that has become synonymous in many other languages with rage—even uncontrollable rage. Amok, however, is extremely rare.

Someone who goes amok loses control over his actions. He—usually a male, although not necessarily—takes whatever weapon comes to hand, often a parang, and blindly mows around him, slashing at people, houses, animals, trees—anything that is in his path.

Malays say he is blind (*mata gelap,* literally "eyes in darkness"), he cannot even see where he is going; he weaves like a drunk, sometimes he falls, he stumbles over pebbles.

What do people do with a person who has gone amok? the visitor wanted to know?

The driver turned to us again: "Oh, it is dangerous to come too close in the beginning of his amok, so people run away. Later on they always catch him."

"And then?" the psychologist asked. "Do they punish him?"

No, they would not punish him. Why would they punish him for being blind? The driver added that he had not heard of an amok in many years. "But today," he added, almost sadly, "the police would probably catch him and then he would go to jail."

The psychologist wanted to know whether there were any programs to treat amok or other mental illnesses. "Or perhaps there is even prevention?"

No, not that we knew.

Malays kept their mentally ill to themselves—and they did not think of them as ill. Some people behave one way, others behave differently, but they are all people of our kampong.

Afterword

No truth can make another truth untrue.
All knowledge is part of the whole knowledge.
Once you have seen the larger pattern,
You cannot go back to seeing the part as the whole.

Ursula K. Le Guin,
Four Ways to Forgiveness

I consider myself fortunate indeed to have spent the first twenty-some years of my life in countries where more than one language was spoken (none of them English). From the time when I first learned to talk, I knew that some people in my environment not only spoke different words, but they also used words differently. As I learned two languages simultaneously, nobody told me that I must speak one language to my parents and another to other people. As all children do, I *knew* without having to be told.

Children learn a language not from a book, or even from a teacher, but from their need to communicate. Learning two languages—especially when they are very different—made me learn two words for the same thing, but more often two different ways to talk about what only seemed to be the same thing.

One language fitted the way my parents and other Westerners saw the world; another language fitted the different way people of the country saw their world. That was never remarkable to me when I was a child; today I realize that untaught learning was a great gift. It is quite unremarkable to me now to know that any language expresses a unique way of knowing.

We in the West know our world from seeing, hearing, and measuring what we assume to be a complex thing with many parts. We rarely use any of the other five senses we recognize to know reality.

In other areas of the world people know from *experiencing* their world as a living, organic whole, where everything relates to everything and where we blend in as but another part of that whole. That experience is not seeing, or hearing, or measuring—it is a direct experiencing of all that we are.

Naturally, Western languages express a Western view of reality. Westerners think of their language too as a thing, a container of words and meanings in which the words are parts and grammar defines and determines the relationship between words. In other parts of the world a language is thought to be the voice of the organism that is the Whole, as birdsong is, or the roar of a waterfall. Those languages often have (at least had) no written form and therefore no officially fixed grammar. Such aspects of language as word order, the function of verbs, the kind and number of relationships that are recognized, and even the tone in which a certain sound is produced can be much more flexible, fluent, and free. To us such a language may seem poetic, because we associate poetry with a differently structured use of words.

✺ ✺

Knowing the different feelings of languages so obviously related to different views of reality has made it easier for me to understand and appreciate people who have very different points of view—which means different assumptions about what is good and what is proper, and particularly different assumptions of what *is*.

The stories in this book are about people who have worldviews different from the Western one. They know their world differently. We do not question that a hospital is the right place to take a seriously ill patient. For people who think about illness and even death differently from the way we do, the Western way of thinking about illness and death may be very difficult to accept. That is not heartless or stupid; it is simply another way of thinking about important events in life. Different values are not wrong, just different.

The way people perceive and structure their reality is expressed in their language. It is difficult to convey the depth and the *feel* of one language in the words of another. The dialogues in these stories are written in English, but they were spoken in Malay, Sng'oi, or Dutch, and some other languages as well. They may even have been spoken in a kind of English that most Americans might not easily recognize as English! My translation into English words and an English sentence structure can only clumsily represent another view of reality.

❈ ❈

Even though I may have *known* when I grew up, I am deeply grateful to the friends in many parts of the world who helped me regain that core of my being, the knowing that I am an inseparable part of this earth. Again I feel one with plants and animals, the sun and the moon. Atoms of my body were once part of a bird, a lava rock, water, before I got to use them. My spirit is fed by Tiger, by a tree, an orange-violet sunrise over the Pacific, the power of a storm.

I sense your pain and your joy because they are mine as well.

I do not *believe* this. I did not choose this. I *know* it as a given. Deep inside I always knew, but so much that I learned smothered that knowing. The friends of these stories helped me recover my heritage.

✠ ✠

A few years ago, a friend of the family and I spent a day at a beach in Kona on the Big Island of Hawai'i. As we were slowly crossing a very rocky area on the way to the beach, one step at a time for fear of sliding or falling, I picked up a perfect, whole cowrie shell. Cowries are not rare, but a whole Lowrie shell, without holes or scrapes, is. This one was at least two inches across and did not seem to have a blemish.

I carried the shell with me to the beach, where we sat down and spent a long day talking. I caressed the shell as we talked, my fingers memorizing its wonderfully complex curves, my eyes imprinting its subtle colors.

Gunga probably did most of the talking; he often does. Gunga—not his name, but it is what we call him—is almost pure Hawaiian. He has little education and cannot read or write. He is fiercely proud of his heritage, and, as do most Hawaiians, he loves the Land, the *'aina*—which means much more than land. 'Aina also means something like "home," or "life-giver," the ground of one's existence. He and his extended family once owned the land they lived on and from, but through trickery, misunderstandings, and various other ploys that are legal in our Western system of justice, they no longer own much of anything—least of all the land.

When we were ready to go home, I carefully put the shell back among the rocks, close to where I had found it.

Gunga stopped in his tracks and said with surprise: "Eh, you no *haole* [white person]; haole always want own everything they see or touch." He shook his head, mumbling all the way back to the car, "Boy, he no haole, putting that shell back on the beach. . . . Eh, he no haole . . ."

The cowrie shell is precious in its own setting. Apart from the ocean, the beach, the sun, a shell is but a thing.

For a long time I cherished in my heart the stories collected in this book because I feared what would happen if they were taken out of context, like a shell taken away from the ocean and the sun.

It is difficult for Westerners to accept that people and their worlds are inseparable. Now all ancient worlds are threatened by our greed, our machines, our civilization. A young Sng'oi man told me the People are dying out; others have told me they have no place to run to anymore. As Hawaiians say, *Ha'ina mai ka puana*—Let the story be told!

A friend said to me, "You were lucky; you had an unusual childhood."

In many ways my childhood was much like the childhood of the great majority of people of this world. My friend's childhood, growing up in America, was more unusual than mine. I grew up in a world and at a time when people touched each other, when we knew animals and plants intimately. It was only later, when I lived in the

Western world, became educated, and lived through a war that I began to feel alienated from the earth and from my fellow humans. I was told to be in charge of my life, rather than live it. I must fight to survive, they assured me. They said the world is a jungle—but when I again knew the jungle, I knew that the jungle of wild Life is not at all like the jungle of Western civilization, and certainly not as dangerous.

For many years I had to work so hard to do the things I was supposed to do that I became deaf and blind to what is important inside me. My luck was to find people who were human in an ancient way. My luck was to recognize and reclaim a humanity rooted in the earth.

All who are in touch with the natural world can sense energies, emotions, and intentions of people and animals. If we listen, we can know—all we need to do is give up being in charge. *Knowing* inside is not something unusual; it is how we are. All humans can have that connection with All-That-Is. The connection is within us.

May these stories help others remember.

Volcano, Hawai'i, 2001